The Venice Report

Demography, Tourism, Financing and Change of Use of Buildings

Jane Da Mosto
Thierry Morel, University of Cambridge
Renato Gibin, Università IUAV, Venice
Stefania Tonin, Università IUAV, Venice
Fabrizio Fracchia, Università Bocconi, Milan
Roberto Agnoletto, Università Bocconi, Milan
Francesca Mattassoglio, Università Bocconi, Milan
Lidia Panzeri
Anna Somers Cocks, Venice in Peril Fund
Tom Spencer, Coastal Research Unit, University of Cambridge
Enrico Tantucci, La Nuova Venezia

CAMBRIDGE
UNIVERSITY PRESS

Authors
Jane Da Mosto
Thierry Morel, University of Cambridge
Renato Gibin, Università IUAV, Venice
Stefania Tonin, Università IUAV, Venice
Fabrizio Fracchia, Università Bocconi, Milan
Roberto Agnoletto, Università Bocconi, Milan
Francesca Mattassoglio, Università Bocconi, Milan
Lidia Panzeri
Anna Somers Cocks, Venice in Peril Fund
Tom Spencer, Coastal Research Unit, University of Cambridge
Enrico Tantucci, La Nuova Venezia

Steering Committee
Marcial Echenique, Professor of Land Use and Transport Studies, Department of
Architecture, University of Cambridge
John Hooper, The Guardian newspaper
Deborah Howard, Professor of Architectural History, Department of Architecture,
University of Cambridge
Francis Phillimore, Trustee, Venice in Peril Fund
Anna Somers Cocks, Chairman, Venice in Peril Fund

Editing by Nigel Reynolds
Editorial coordination by Tamara Risso-Gill
Graphic design by Ellen Carpenter, Shakeup Media
Photographs by Katherine Hardy, Sarah Quill, Brian Sibley, Raffaella Toffolo, David Weeks
Translating by Ros Schwartz Translations Ltd

Cover image © Raffaella Toffolo

Acknowledgements
Charles Aldington, Deutsche Bank; Alessio Altichieri; Nicky Baly, Development Director,
Venice in Peril; Stefano Boato, Università IUAV, Venice; Context Travel; Luigi D'Alpaos,
University of Padua; Armando Danella, Consultant on the Special Law, Municipality
of Venice; Brian Ferme, Istituto di Diritto Canonico San Pio X, Venice; Antonio Foscari,
Università IUAV, Venice; Pierfrancesco Ghetti, Ca' Foscari University, Venice; David
Landau, Trustee, Venice in Peril Fund; Cornelia Lauf, Università IUAV, Venice; Silvia Meloni,
Consorzio Venezia Nuova; Stefano Micelli, Isabella Scaramuzzi, Giuseppina di Monte
and their teams, COSES, Venice; John Millerchip, Trustee, Venice in Peril Fund; Marina
Morrisson Atwater, Trustee, Venice in Peril Fund; Ignazio Musu, Venice International
University; Lidia Panzeri; PizzaExpress; Sarah Quill, Trustee, Venice in Peril Fund; Pilar
Rivett Bertuzzi, Goldman Sachs; Clare Robson; Jacob Rothschild; Mara Rumiz, Assessore
for Public Works, Housing and Heritage, Municipality of Venice; Alex Saz-Carranza,
Deutsche Bank; Cristiana Scarpa, Environment Department, Municipality of Venice;
Jessica Thomas; Carla Toffolo, Association of Private Committees for Venice, Venice;
Venice Simplon - Orient-Express; Stefano Vignani, Direttore Marittimo del Veneto; Ted
Wake, Kirker Holidays

**Published with the financial support of
The TLTC Conservation Foundation**

The Venice in Peril Fund
The British Committee for the Preservation of Venice
Unit 4, Hurlingham Studios, Ranelagh Gardens, London SW6 3PA
Tel: +44 (0) 20 7736 6891 Fax: +44 (0) 20 7751 0738
info@veniceinperil.org   www.veniceinperil.org
Registered Charity Number 262146

Katherine Hardy © Venice in Peril

TABLE OF CONTENTS

Introduction
Page 7

Chapter 1
Venice: its demography
Page 10

Chapter 2
Venice on the mainland
Page 22

Chapter 3
Tourism
Page 30

Chapter 4
Changes of use of buildings
Page 46

Chapter 5
Public funding: is the future of Venice sustainable?
Page 86

Bibliography
Page 104

INTRODUCTION

**By Anna
Somers Cocks**

The chapters of the Venice Report, commissioned by Venice in Peril in collaboration with the Department of Architecture of Cambridge University, reveal that things are changing fast in Venice. After the great flood of 1966 until early this century, Venice became a city where policy was made very cautiously, where the authorities seemed to prefer to do nothing, or even oppose action, rather than do the wrong thing. Hence the many years it took for MOSE, the mobile flood barriers, to begin to be built. The Arsenale, the obsolete naval dockyard, is another case in point. After 50 years, the only, very limited, progress in adapting it to new use has taken place when outside private or semi-private bodies, the Biennale and the Consorzio Venezia Nuova, have twisted the arm of the authorities.

Lately, however, Italy has been trying to liberalise its economy and the dirigiste power of Rome has diminished as the regions have negotiated greater autonomy. The reduction in public funding has also been very influential. In Venice, the key moment was 2002, when the go-ahead was finally given for MOSE. On the one hand, Venice will be protected from the acque alte after 2014, its expected completion date. On the other, the lavish cushion of money that the Comune used to enjoy from the Special Laws for Venice has grown a great deal thinner, perhaps too thin, if work on maintaining the canals and fabric of Venice is put at risk. The current mayor, Massimo Cacciari, talks constantly about his lack of funds, justifying the huge ads in St Mark's Square and the proposal to put Coca Cola vending machines in the calli and campi on those grounds.

Venice is a fertile forcing house; it is remarkable how quickly growth has come as soon as the private sector has been given its head. In just seven years, the number of B&Bs and rooms to rent has risen 1008 per cent. The number of cruise ships sailing through Venice has risen from 200 to 510 a year since 2000, facilitated by the privatization of the passenger port management. Five years ago Venice was a city without noticeable advertising; now huge ads appear on most public buildings under restoration. Venice, whose economy is mysterious because so much of it is undeclared, nevertheless is estimated by CISET, a research

body at Ca'Foscari University, to turn over €1.5 billion a year. Venice is a cash cow for Venetians, but increasingly also for outside interests.

The Venice Report describes the plans for a very big development at Tessera, around the airport. This is not only to have a huge hotel by prestige architect Frank Gehry, but a casino, shopping centres and a stadium. It is as much directed at the mainland as at Venice, but the guaranteed attraction of the Serenissima, the apparently endless curiosity to see this city, certainly encourages the investors. Could this be a kind of antechamber to Venice, where tourists would stay, and, as the economist John Kay suggested in his speech to the Istituto Veneto in 2008, pass through a didactic preparation for the transcendent experience of sailing down the Grand Canal? Or will it be an economic machine

Venice is at a **crossroads**: **choices now** could be decisive, for **good or for very bad**

dependant on forcing more and more people into the already crowded calli of the historic city?

Not for nothing does the airport have shares in the passenger port of Venice, which boasts of generating 10 per cent of the tourist economy of the city. Not for nothing is this port expanding; expect to see even more vast cruise ships dwarfing the Piazzetta of St Mark.

None of the above is irreversible, but the plans for a commercial port and transport hub, big enough to rival Trieste, at Marghera on edge of the lagoon would almost certainly be permanent in its effect on the city. Such a port would be very welcome for the mainland economy because the petrochemical works there are obsolescent, and central government is looking for an alternative source of employment to be able to cease subsidizing them.

But to make such a port economic requires the deep dredging of the channel from the Malamocco inlet to Marghera to let in the big bulk carriers, and it is precisely these deep channels that over the years contributed, with other environmental factors, to the degradation of the lagoon and the chronically raised water levels in the city. There is a great deal of scientific research and consensus on this matter, so it cannot just be brushed aside. The Autorità Portuale, in its submission to the Italian Senate this May about this project, not only ignores this evidence, but makes a completely unproven statement: "the situation regarding the lagoon is completely changed and the problem of its hydraulic equilibrium is solved because it will be possible to manage it through judicious use of the MOSE system". And with that statement, which confuses the role of MOSE in defending Venice from flooding events with the question of the degradation of the lagoon, the submission dispatches all the environmental risk to Venice of the port development project.

Who can speak up for Venice in such a situation? The mayor of Venice cannot be any more than a lobbyist with central government as he or she has no legal control over what happens with the port, it being an autonomous public body of the state. There is the Comitatone (big committee) for major policy decisions regarding Venice, made up of government ministers and representatives of local government, and presided over by the prime minister. But in Silvio Berlusconi's government, with its belief in big infrastructure projects,

disregard for the environment and its political indebtedness to north east Italy, the Comitatone is unlikely to favour caution. And neither is the project likely to be opposed by the electorate of Venice, as only 30 per cent of it inhabits the historic city and lagoon islands, while 70 per cent is on the mainland and is more likely to benefit in the short term from the developments.

Of course, the whole economy of the Veneto, indeed of Italy, benefits from Venice, one of the greatest tourist attractions in the world, but this seems to be so taken for granted that it is not explicitly part of the political discussion. It is therefore indispensable and urgent that a realistic study (also taking account of the black economy) gets carried out, showing who spends the money and who benefits.

Especially now that a greater degree of free enterprise is being allowed in and around Venice, two basic economic tools also need to be applied by the authorities —and investors: risk assessment (particularly where the plans for the port are concerned) and cost-benefit analysis. For example, is it worth investing billions in a port and transport hub if, as a consequence, you have to spend billions longterm protecting the buildings of Venice from the water? Is it worth bringing in more and more day-trippers if they crowd out the tourists who stay at least one night in Venice and spend more money there?

It is exciting to see that the latest, excellent study by the research group COSES has for the first time, and at the request of the Comune (municipality), worked out what the maximum number of tourists in Venice might be (86,000 a day, but they do not recommend it).

It is fascinating reading for anyone who has experienced alley-rage in one of the main routes through Venice; the Tourism Chapter describes its methodology and gives a summary of its findings. This is the first sign that the Comune is thinking of how to manage the numbers of visitors, rather than continuing with the laissez-faire policy it has defended hitherto. The question is whether they will be able make the investors in the business interests around Venice into allies, so that a policy bringing dividends in the long rather than the short term will prevail. Nobody should forget: the prize is the most beautiful city on earth, one of the most marvelous creations of man. That is beyond price.

SUMMARY

● The officially resident population of the historic city of Venice is 60,209, barely a third of 60 years ago. Although the water city is still the seat of the Veneto regional government and the Comune's offices are still next to the Rialto Bridge, the reality is that with its dwindling voter base representing only 20% of the whole municipality, the historic city and its interests sway the elections less than the interests of the mainland.

● But the city is not "dying" for lack of inhabitants, as frequently stated; besides the officially registered residents, it has 15,000 people living at least sporadically in second homes and around 4,000 residing students.

● A new, important study of tourism in Venice has come up with the first assessment of how many tourists the city can hold comfortably and safely; a minimum of 31,000 if the tourist industry is to keep going, with 86,000 as the disagreeable saturation point (in 2007, 59,000 visitors came to Venice). An online incentive/disincentive advance booking scheme, Venice Connected, run by the Comune is a first step towards managing the flow.

● Government funds for running and maintaining the historic city have diminished sharply. Since 2002, much of special government funding Venice used to receive has been diverted towards the building of MOSE, the mobile flood barriers that are expected to cost €4.271 billion. So while the Comune received €592 million extra in 2002, in 2007, it was only €133 million. This means that vital maintenance such as the dredging and repair of canals may slow down. Central government funding for the maintenance of listed buildings has also been cut, by 25.8% in 2009, which is the reason the authorities give for having allowed huge adverts to appear on iconic buildings such as the Doge's Palace.

● Over the last five to 10 years, the private sector has begun to play a far bigger role in the future of the city. Planning laws have been liberalized to allow private homes to be turned into B&Bs and rooms to rent. On the one hand, this has ensured the maintenance of these buildings, on the other it has reduced the number of habitations available to residents by about 420 units and has contributed to the doubling of property prices since 2000, further encouraging residents to leave. The airport and passenger port of Venice, both run by private companies, are planning major expansions on the basis of growth in tourist traffic. The number of cruise ships sailing through Venice was 200 in 2000 but 510 in 2007, and the number of berths for the big ships is being increased.

● There are plans for a huge expansion around the airport and of the commercial port of Venice at Marghera on the mainland, partly to replace the economy of the obsolescent chemical factories there. The size of the investment required would consolidate the need to keep the lagoon channels dredged to a depth of at least 12 m when there is good scientific evidence that these deep channels are one of the causes of the degradation of the Venice lagoon, which is damaging to the historic city.

Chapter 1
Venice: Its Demography

Jane Da Mosto

- The officially registered population of the historic city of Venice is 60,028, barely a third of what it was 60 years ago

- This dwindling number means that the historic city has lost power in the elected municipality of Venice. The voters are now divided 20:10:70 between the historic city, the lagoon islands and the mainland

- There are many more stakeholders than just the registered citizens and the city should not be written off as a mere tourist destination

- Commuters, students and tourists double the resident population every day

1
INTRODUCTION

What is the population of Venice? The bare statistics collected by the Comune's ufficio anagrafe, the municipal registry office, paint a bleak picture of a "dying city" where the officially measured resident population has been in steady and serious decline for more than half a century.

In March 2009, the number of registered residents of the historic city was 60,208, with a further 30,362 living in Venice's islands and estuary. This gives a total of 90,570 people designated as permanent residents of the "lagoon city", a term to embrace the historic city, the Lido, Pellestrina and the islands of the lagoon.

The ufficio anagrafe keeps a record of all residents living in the municipality: all Italian citizens are required to register their place of permanent residence from the moment of birth, as well as foreigners who are officially living in Italy. The figures record all other demographic changes such as births, marriages and deaths, household composition and immigration and emigration.

Taken alone, the municipality's official figures would appear to confirm the widely held belief that Venice is shrinking: since 1952 when the number of residents of the "lagoon city" peaked at 218,991, the permanent registered population has diminished by more than 60 per cent and steadily continues its decline. It has shrunk by a further nine per cent since the beginning of the century or an average of 1,000 people per annum.

The officially resident population of the historic city shows an even more marked fall, from a peak of 174,808 in 1951 to 60,208 in March 2008.

But is this the whole picture? Far from it. The real population of Venice is much more complex and many other people also "inhabit" the city in ways that are more or less stable. They, too, need to be considered in any realistic analysis of the city's demography for the purposes of planning, providing services and policy-making.

The main categories – leaving aside the numerous tourists and day-trippers who collectively make heavy demands on the city's infrastructure – include people with secondary homes, commuting workers, students and the steady flow of people who come to Venice to use its public administration offices, since Venice is the regional capital, and hospitals or are members of the army and navy stationed in the city as well as prison inmates.

In 1994, the Venice Comune first attempted to estimate and evaluate the population from this perspective; another study was published in 2006 (using data from 2004) and most recently, a 2007

[1] *Una stima della popolazione presente nel Comune di Venezia – Anno 2004, Comune di Venezia, Ufficio Statistica, Venice 2006*

RISE AND FALL OF THE RESIDENT POPULATION
Resident population of Venice, 1871 to 2008

- ● Historic city
- ● Islands of the lagoon
- ● Lagoon (incl. historic city)
- ○ Mainland Venice
- ● Comune of Venice

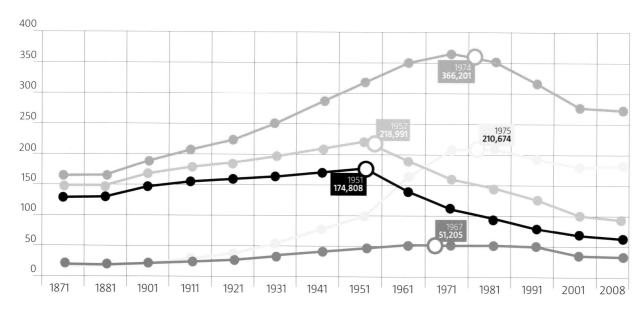

The historic city is particularly **densely populated**, **7,558 inhabitants/km2** if the open waters of the lagoon are excluded

RISE AND FALL OF THE
RESIDENT POPULATION
Resident population of
Venice, 1871 to 2008

YEAR	HISTORIC CITY (a)	LAGOON ISLANDS (b)	a + b	MAINLAND VENICE (c)	TOTAL FOR COMUNE OF VENICE
1871	128787	19457	148244	16356	164600
1881	129851	18512	148363	17045	165408
1901	146682	21064	167746	20597	188343
1911	154891	23670	178561	28580	207141
1921	159262	26769	186031	37419	223450
1931	163559	32826	196385	53937	250322
1951	174808	44037	218845	96966	315811
1952	174448	44543	218991	100124	319115
1953	172195	45368	217563	105018	322581
1954	170446	45875	216321	110232	326553
1955	167069	46615	213684	115777	329461
1956	162834	47126	209960	122015	331975
1957	158466	47624	206090	129629	335719
1958	154268	48120	202388	137469	339857
1959	150242	48823	199065	145282	344347
1960	145402	49025	194427	152575	347002
1961	137150	49702	186852	161035	347887
1962	132148	50026	182174	168201	350375
1963	129468	50099	179567	176094	355661
1964	126808	50388	177196	183045	360241
1965	123733	51079	174812	188907	363719
1966	121309	51125	172434	193314	365748
1967	118889	51205	170094	196720	366814
1968	116270	51117	167387	200445	367832
1969	113587	51142	164729	202902	367631
1970	111550	50729	162279	205249	367528
1971	108429	48747	157173	205829	363002
1972	106516	49339	155855	207685	363540
1973	106806	49755	156561	209640	366201
1974	105656	49864	155520	209911	365431
1975	104206	49670	153876	210674	364550
1976	102269	49713	151982	210512	362494
1977	100608	49690	150298	209995	360293
1978	99189	49642	148831	209435	358266
1979	97280	49632	146912	208953	355865
1980	95222	49420	144642	207811	352453
1981	93598	49203	142801	206707	349663
1982	92118	49295	141413	204817	346391
1983	90414	49108	139522	203115	342798
1984	87936	48885	136821	201429	338416
1985	86072	48584	134656	200084	334932
1986	84355	48317	132672	198577	331454
1987	82703	47972	130675	196851	327700
1988	80988	47676	128664	195498	324294
1989	79487	47480	126967	193894	320990
1990	78165	47271	125436	192270	317837
1991	76644	47057	123701	190136	313967
1992	75159	46911	122070	187783	309982
1993	73149	46448	119597	184885	304486
1994	72037	46186	118223	183294	301529
1995	71053	45840	116893	182072	298967
1996	69906	45651	115557	180899	296459
1997	68600	45382	113982	179745	293731
1998	67838	45063	112901	178630	291531
1999	66945	32845	99790	177515	277305
2000	66386	32451	98837	176531	275368
2001	65695	32183	97878	176290	274168
2002	64076	31767	95843	174915	270758
2003	63947	31670	95617	176046	271663
2004	63353	31393	94746	176505	271251
2005	62296	31035	93331	176449	269780
2006	61611	30702	92313	176621	268934
2007	60755	30589	91344	177649	268993
2008	60311	30415	90726	179372	270098

[2] Di Monte G. and Santoro G.,
Venezia: quartiere metropolitano,
COSES Doc. 1032.0, October 2008

study, updated in 2008 by COSES (the Consortium for Research and Educational Training, a research study centre established by the City and Province of Venice) concluded that the number of people present in Venice on an average day is 143,450 including the tourists .

This is over 50 per cent more than the total resident population of "lagoon city" and over 100 per cent more than the number of residents in the historic city, where the bulk of this transient population goes.

This concept of "popolazione presente", or the effective population, has grown in importance and become a common method for studying issues concerning large metropolises and urban sociology. The increased mobility of people means that the actual human load on a city is much larger (and of a different nature) than that created solely by residents and it needs to be measured and described.

To understand what this level of human pressure means to Venice, it is more meaningful to convert the annual number for effective population (used for economic statistics) to an equivalent population figure, which gives a better idea of the number of people in Venice on a typical day of the year (but does not take account of seasonal variations), for planning purposes such as the calibration of city services. So, here we are getting much nearer to a definition of the real population of Venice, one that considers the inhabitants of Venice in a wider sense and that encompasses as many as possible of the city's stakeholders.

The shrinking number of permanent residents, though a serious issue, pales in comparison to the global importance of the city, its heritage and the number of transient "city users" and leisure visitors.

2
BREAKING DOWN THE POPULATION

Permanent residents

The officially resident population of the Comune of Venice (the municipality) is distributed in a ratio of approximately 20:10:70 between the historic city, the islands and the mainland (only the officially resident are allowed to vote). This demographic fact means that in electoral terms, the historic city is now in the minority. When local politicians refer to "Venezia", they are no longer referring to the Venice the world thinks of as Venice, but to a terraferma/lagoon hybrid, in which the terraferma has the political clout.

The total population of the municipality reached its peak in 1968 at 367,832. Although the population of the historic city was declining by then, industrialisation at Marghera on the edge of the lagoon was flourishing. Population in the lagoon on the islands and the estuary areas also continued growing until the late 1960s, particularly as a result of thriving glass production on the island of Murano.

More recently, the population of the lagoon (the

258/ inhabitants per km2 while the national average is 195/km2. But there is great variability in the "lagoon city", ranging from a single priest residing on the island of San Francesco del Deserto to the 17,509 official residents of Cannaregio, a neighbourhood in the historic city.

There are more official residents on the island of Murano (4,776) than in the sestiere (district) of San Marco (4,257), which is considered to be the "heart" of Venice. And the island of Burano has more residents (2,917) than the sestiere of Sant'Elena.

The mainland has a higher share of births since it also has more immigrants from outside Italy, a sector of the population characterised by larger families. Foreigners (over 40 per cent from Eastern Europe and over 30 per cent from Asian countries) also contribute to lowering the average age since mostly they are of working age (25-44 years old).

Deaths outnumber births

The mainland has a higher share of births than the rest of Venice since it also has more immigrants from outside Italy, including nationalities characterised by large families. Foreigners (over 40 per cent from Eastern Europe and over 30 per cent from Asian countries) have also contributed to lowering the average age in the municipality of Venice, since most newcomers are of working age (25-44 years old), according to the statistics department of the Comune of Venice.

Since 2000, the average number of births per year has been 705 for the "lagoon city" (472 in the historic city and 233 on the islands) and 2,113 for municipality. Over the same period, the annual death rate is 1,387 for the "lagoon city" (970 and 417 in the historic city and the islands respectively) and 3,329 for the municipality.Both annual rates have been relatively stable for a number of years and it is the gap between them, along with the continuing exodus from Venice that is causing the decline in the city's population.

The Venice Lagoon

Italy

BOUNDARIES OF THE COMUNE OF VENICE

historic city, the Lido, Pellestrina and the islands) has fallen by more than a third (since 1981), double the rate of the decrease on the mainland areas of Venice.

Population distribution is patchy
The historic city is particularly densely populated: 7,558 inhabitants/km2 if the open waters of the lagoon are excluded and not counting the islands, which have 1,616 inhabitants per km^{23}. By contrast, the population density of the Veneto region is

[3] *Serie storica della densità demografica per località: residenti per kmq, acque escluse (1998-2008),* Comune di Venezia, Ufficio Statistica, Venice 2009

Katherine Hardy © Venice in Peril

THE SESTIERI OF VENICE
*The six districts of the
historic city*

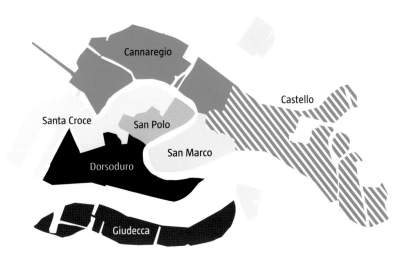

Cannaregio

Castello

Santa Croce

San Polo

San Marco

Dorsoduro

Giudecca

Emigration and immigration

The population is apparently very mobile. Taking annual figures since 2000, the greatest outflow has been to the mainland where housing is cheaper and employment opportunities are greater. More people leave Venice to live elsewhere in Venice province or in the Veneto region than come to the city from these areas, resulting in a net average loss of 1,046 people (to the province) and 458 (to the region) per annum.

To set against this, there has been a net inflow of 1,769 people each year from abroad (and of 253 people from other regions of Italy). Most of the foreigners do not settle in the "lagoon city" but in the mainland area of Venice municipality.

The top five countries of origin are Albania (12.3%), Romania (11.8%), Bangladesh (8.7%), Moldavia (7.4%) and Morocco (7.3%).

The proportion of women varies according to country of origin. Nearly all the arrivals from

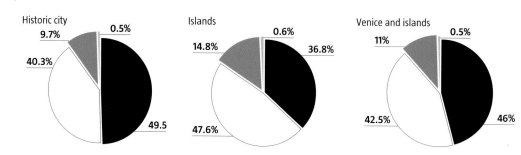

HOUSEHOLD SIZES
● Single person
● 2 and 3 persons
● 4 and 5 persons
○ Over 5 persons

Historic city
9.7%
0.5%
40.3%
49.5

Islands
0.6%
14.8%
36.8%
47.6%

Venice and islands
11%
0.5%
42.5%
46%

Ukraine, Poland, Brazil and Moldavia are women and nearly all from Sri Lanka and Bangladesh are men. This reflects the economic opportunities of the area.

Children form about 20% of the whole. A total of 5.4% of residents of the Comune of Venice are immigrants, while the share is lower, nearer four per cent in the historic city.

The number of households in the Comune with more than two people is 27.5% of the total; among the islands of the lagoon the share is higher at 34%, reflecting the fact that more extended families live together because of the survival of traditional ways of life as well as the limited space on the islands.

Future trends

The decline in the resident population appears set to continue. In 2006, the statistics department of the Comune estimated that by 2015 the total population of the "lagoon city" will fall to 82,653 (55,020 for the historic city and 27,663 in the estuary and islands). This will represent a 9% fall from present levels and a dramatic decline of 16% from the start of this century.

The same forecast predicts that, overall, the Comune will number a total of 258,442 people by 2015, down from 270,098 in the year 2000, which is a 4 per cent drop since the start of the century.

The ageing population

The average age of people living in the historic city is rising sharply. It went up from 40.6 years old (in 1981) to 48.3 (in 2001).

Before 1991, more than 60% of the population came within the 14-59 age bracket, but by 2001 the share had fallen to 58% and the proportion of people aged more than 60 stood at almost 35 per cent, significantly higher than 30 years earlier.

Consequently, the historic city has a disproportionate share of older residents. In 1971, 23.8% of the historic centre's population was aged over 60 (compared to 16.9% in the Comune as a whole). By 2001, the share of over-60s in the historic centre had risen to 34.9% (against 31.3% in the Comune). The Comune predicts that by 2015, the proportion of over-60s overall in the "lagoon city" will have risen to 37%.

The young

Looking to the Venice of the future, the share of the 0-13 age group fell from 16% of total population in the centre in 1971 to 9.1% 30 years later. For the Comune as a whole, the percentage of children under 15 fell from 21.6% to 9.8% over the same period.

It is difficult for the city to calibrate the services, especially education, in line with these trends. At pre-school level (age 3-5), there are 33 nursery schools in the historic city and the islands with places for nearly 2,200 children (2006/7 figures). This is an increase of more than a 10% since 1999/2000. There are 14 elementary schools in Venice and nine on the islands with nearly 3,300 pupils (age 6-10) enrolled for the year 2006/7. This is more than adequate for the historic city but capacity is slightly less than the demand for places on the islands (ie; 94%). For middle school (age 11-13), with 10 establishments, there is excess capacity in the historic centre (116.5%) and undersupply (90.3%) on the islands, which have four schools for this age group. Localised undersupply is not a serious issue as children from the islands can easily attend schools in the main part of the city, since public transport is highly efficient. Since the academic year 1999/2000, the number of children enrolled in these schools has fallen by 2.5% (the historic city) and 6% (the islands).

There are nine high schools, art and technical colleges in Venice with a total of 5,730 students, a fall of 9.4% in five years.

In 2006/7, the mainland had 11 establishments for higher education with a total of 7,753 students, virtually no change on five years earlier. Numbers on the mainland at all levels of schooling appear to have been maintained by the rising numbers of foreigners who have settled there. The share of foreign students in all schools (primary, middle and high schools) was around 11% in 2006/7 compared to 5.7% in the historic city and islands.

15,224 people live in secondary or holiday homes in the "lagoon city", double the number of a decade earlier

Secondary homes

The next most stable category of Venice's stakeholders is citizens normally resident in other parts of Italy or from abroad who have acquired secondary homes in the city. In order to assess the number of homes now inhabited by not officially resident people, we should also include in this category properties that are rented out most of the time, either to a single long-term tenant or to a succession of short-stay visitors in rented self-catering accommodation (often owned by non-residents).

No official figures are collected but it is possible to make an assessment of numbers through the city's utility companies. (See Chapter 3, Change of Use of Buildings.)

Non-resident owned housing in Italy is subject to higher electricity and water rates, so by examining the records of the city's electricity supply company, ENEL, it is not difficult to establish the number of households on the higher (non-residents') tariff. Looking at the average per capita electricity use in these households (average use is considered to be 993 KWs/person on the mainland and 1059 KWs/person in the "lagoon city") it is possible to arrive at the number of non-residents permanently or semi-permanently living in the city.

Figures for 2004 indicated a total of 15,224 people living in secondary homes in the "lagoon city", double the number for a decade earlier. For the entire Comune, the figure in 2004 was 22,894 people.

The true numbers, however, may be somewhat higher. All estimates should be considered as lower estimates.

There is much undeclared activity and employment in the city that is not captured in official data. This has been discovered to be particularly true of tourist-related activities, commuting and undeclared B&B and holiday apartment lets.

Students

This is a very important demographic segment of Venice, not only because of their very large numbers, but also because students form a portion of the effective population that remains "forever young" in the ageing city.

There are more than 25,000 students enrolled in the two universities: over 19,500 at Ca' Foscari University and over 7,000 at the Venice architecture university (IUAV). Both institutions admit around 3,000 and 1,000 new students a year respectively.

The total number of students at Ca' Foscari has oscillated since the early 1990s and for the academic year 2007/8 student numbers were 4.6 per cent lower than 15 years earlier (in 1992/3). IUAV student numbers have fallen more radically over the same period (by 51 per cent).

Course lengths at the two institutions are typically six years. Education reforms introduced a shorter three-year degree course option about 10 years ago but many students still choose to stay on for further specialisation.

Ca' Foscari has four faculties (listed in decreasing order, in terms of student numbers): economics, literature and philosophy, foreign languages and natural sciences. IUAV has three faculties: architecture, design and arts, urban and land use planning.

The Church has three institutions of higher education: the Studium Generale Marcianum, with around 320 students, a number that is expected to rise; the Capuchin Theological Faculty on the Giudecca, with 14 students, and the S. Bernadino Institute of Ecumenical Studies, with 68 students.

There are also other institutions such as the Accademia di Belle Arti (the main art school), the music conservatoire Benedetto Marcello, with more than 600 students, Venice International University (VIU) on the island of San Servolo, which has 250 students on campus throughout the year, as well as a number of Venice-based centres of foreign universities and partnership programmes between Venice universities and others. Ca'Foscari hosts approximately 300 foreign students a year for six to 12 months.

Moreover, the Venice-based programmes of non-Italian universities including Warwick and New York Universities, bring more young people to the city for periods of weeks or months, as well as visiting teaching staff and professors. There are also several international "cultural centres" and institutes for further education that serve hundreds more long term visitors to Venice, notably: the Guggenheim contemporary art course (160 students a year); the

DISTRIBUTION OF CA' FOSCARI STUDENTS
By residence. Figures for the academic year 2008/09

● Venice province
● Padua and Treviso
● Other Veneto provinces
○ The rest of Italy

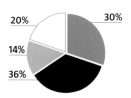

20%
30%
14%
36%

European Centre for Human Rights, S. Niccolò, Lido (90 a term); the Scuola Internazionale di Grafica (100 a year); the Istituto Venezia language school (over 1000 students a year on short courses).

The buildings of the two main universities are distributed around the historic city, rather than being concentrated on campuses. With around 30,000 students and university staff– equivalent to half of the entire resident population of the historic centre – attached to institutions of further education that are mostly in the historic centre, they make a very significant contribution to the effective population.

How many of the students and staff live in Venice full-time — or in term-time, at least —is much harder to determine. Figures for the academic year 2008/9 show that at Ca' Foscari about 30% of all students reside within Venice province and, it is assumed, they live at home, according to information supplied by the Rector's office. 36% come from the neighbouring provinces of Padua and Treviso and could live at home since these places are only a short distance by bus or train from Venice; 14% come from other provinces within the Veneto region and 20% are from the rest of Italy. The share of international students is very low (around 1%) at both Ca' Foscari and IUAV.

At the time of writing, neither university was able to supply information on the number of students who were already Venetian residents (ie; some share of the 30%, or 5,850 individuals, at Ca' Foscari who reside in the province, and 20% in the case of IUAV).

A major study was commissioned in 2004 to better understand the housing needs of Venice's students[4]. More than 18,000 were contacted and 9,794 completed questionnaires were obtained (a 54 per cent response rate), which is considered a stable and reliable result.

The survey found that there were 8000 students who wanted to live in Venice but only 4,600 (less than 60%) had managed to find accommodation, either renting rooms, sharing apartments or staying in university residences, religious institutions etc.

The remaining students said they were actively looking for accommodation in the city or, they would be, if there were a better chance of finding affordable or better quality lodgings.

This unmet demand is the more significant because the survey's respondents also said that living near their place of study not only had logistic advantages but affected university performance (access to libraries, cultural and sporting initiatives, IT facilities etc.). This means that the attractiveness and competitive position of Venice for further education is inextricably linked to accommodation possibilities in the city itself.

The high cost of private sector lodging in Venice is clearly a very important obstacle limiting growth of the student population in Venice. More than 60% of resident students pay rent of more than €200 per month plus expenses; yet two-thirds of students who said that they were looking for lodgings declared that they would not be prepared to pay this much and 43% (including students who were not actively looking for accommodation in Venice but would like to live there) said that it was not worth the effort of looking for lodgings in the city because of high rents.

At a recent meeting on student housing in Venice, Mara Rumiz, who is in charge of housing and public works for the Comune, said that while the local administration was very concerned about the lack of student accommodation, it could do nothing to help directly since its priority was to develop housing for permanent residents.

[4] Mantovan Pietro, Pastore Andrea and Tonellato Stefano, *Gli Alloggi per Studenti Universitari a Venezia: risultati dell'indagine 2004 promossa da Co.Ca.I sulla condizione residenziale degli studenti degli atenei veneziani*, Dipartimento di Statistica, Università Ca' Foscari, Venezia, ottobre 2005

Commuters

A major component of Venice's daytime population is commuters, those who work in the city, those who visit regularly to use its services and the numerous students who do not live in the municipality.

It is, of course, open to debate to what extent this transient presence should be considered part of the permanent population since, by definition, they live elsewhere, either on the mainland part of Venice or beyond its boundaries, and therefore they do not have any direct stake in Venice in the form of voting powers or by owning property. Yet they still depend on its transport infrastructure, use many other services and contribute to varying degrees in the local economy, not least, by making Venice their place of work.

The most reliable information on this regular influx comes from the latest census of 2001. It found that 62,222 people commuted into Venice every day (students and workers) and 17,414

[5] Di Monte G. and Santoro G. (Eds), Venezia – *Porte di Accesso alla Città Antica*, COSES Doc. 929.0, October 2007

commuted out of the city, meaning a daily daytime net increase of 44,408 people in Venice. Taking into account holiday periods, the average daily presence of commuters would be 36,728[5].

Unfortunately, there is no way to get a more recent and accurate picture of commuting because of the large number of variables influencing the sale of travel season tickets.

The data provided by the train authorities, for example, is insufficiently broken down; some commuters do not use public transport to get

Detail of the Palazzo Soranzo Piovene

to Venice nor to travel within Venice, and some temporary visitors buy season tickets for the vaporettos.

The real number of commuters – and therefore their contribution to the effective population - is bound to be much larger than the census figure because of the flow of temporary and black-market workers, especially in tourism-related, bar and restaurant activities, which have grown sharply in recent years and because of others who periodically need to visit Venice.

3
CONCLUSIONS

The effective daily population of the historic city of Venice is more than double that of the officially registered residents.

We have seen that by 2008, these official residents in the historic city had fallen to 60,311, to 90,726 in the "lagoon city" (the centre, the islands, the Lido and Pellestrina) and to 270,098 living in the whole municipality of Venice.

But using almost comparable figures, the 2006 statistics analysed by COSES[6], the real number of people using the city's shops, streets, transport and sewage system every day puts a much greater load on the infrastructure.

Counting all residents, commuters, tourists, students, secondary home owners, visitors renting flats or staying in B&Bs, and others, the effective daily population of the "lagoon city" of Venice – ie; the historic city, the islands, the Lido and Pellestrina – was 184,000 in 2006, according to COSES.

The table below summarizes the different types of people present in Venice in terms of total numbers and also converts these figures into a daily effective number, based on assumptions about the average annual number of trips to Venice or length of stay.

It is strikingly evident that a large number of people "occupy" Venice at all times of the year.

[6] Pedenzini C and Mantese E., *Bilancio Demografico Provinciale, Anno 2006*, COSES Doc. 916, September 2007

VENICE'S EFFECTIVE DAYTIME POPULATION
COSES 2007, based on data from 2006

● Total number
● Daily effective number

Venice and Islands

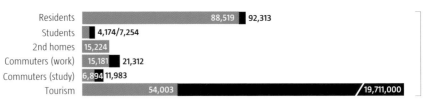

	Total number	Daily effective number
Residents	92,313	88,519
Students	7,254	4,174
2nd homes	15,224	
Commuters (work)	21,312	15,181
Commuters (study)	11,983	6,894
Tourism	19,711,000	54,003

Effective daily population: 184,000

Mainland

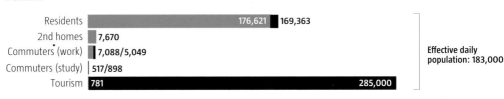

	Total number	Daily effective number
Residents	169,363	176,621
2nd homes	7,670	
Commuters (work)	7,088	5,049
Commuters (study)	517	898
Tourism	285,000	781

Effective daily population: 183,000

Total Comune

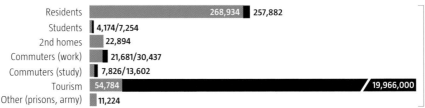

	Total number	Daily effective number
Residents	257,882	268,934
Students	7,254	4,174
2nd homes	22,894	
Commuters (work)	30,437	21,681
Commuters (study)	13,602	7,826
Tourism	19,966,000	54,784
Other (prisons, army)	11,224	

Effective daily population: 380,500

© Sarah Quill

Anyone can see that it is far from the dying or abandoned city that the falling numbers of permanent residents alone would suggest.

This is a reality not just for Venice but for many cities around the world that are increasingly populated by transient flows of people for work and leisure. It seems to be time, therefore, to start redefining the way the city is occupied and the many types of stakeholder involved.

Cultural diversity and a changing population have always been integral to the history of Venice. Its resident population has been marked by sharp oscillations yet has always remained resilient. In the past, parts of the city were left empty when the population went into decline. Today, the picture is very different. Strong demand for property and space indicates only that permanent residents are being displaced by other types of city user and tourists.

The loss of political influence in the municipal elections due to the small number of voters in the historic city may have long-reaching implications for policy decisions about the city, which is increasingly unable to counter outside interest groups.

The public administration needs to get a clearer breakdown of Venice's user groups to better understand where synergies and conflicts emerge in their competing demands on the infrastructure, economy, architecture, cultural heritage and environment.

Calibration of city services, notably sanitation, public hygiene and transport, needs to take account of these different user groups and allocate the costs appropriately.

While the larger effective population in Venice puts pressure on utilities, for example accounting for over 40% of urban waste collection, it also provides the critical mass needed for some basic services such as vaporetto routes that could not be justified by the resident population alone.

Chapter 2
Venice on the
mainland

Enrico Tantucci
Tom Spencer

1

VENICE ON THE MAINLAND

By Enrico Tantucci

Venice is like Manhattan—a borough, albeit the most famous, in a much larger metropolitan city stretching as far as Padua and Treviso—but no longer an autonomous city. For its administrators, that is what Venice is today (population 60,000 and falling), as described by COSES, the Consortium for Research and for Educational Training whose data the Comune (Municipality) uses in making its strategic decisions. These decisions are largely taken outside Venice now, and frequently are imposed by, or at best negotiated with, private investors because Venice no longer has the funds to plan its own future.

The key event has been central government's severe cuts to the funds it used to give to the Comune under the Special Law for Venice (in 2002, Venice drew down €592 million under this arrangement. In 2005, the figure dropped to just €23 million although it had picked up to €133 million in 2007 (see Chapter 5, Finance)) that guaranteed the money needed for the maintenance of the city on water, for the dredging and repair of its canals and for the restoration of its buildings. Public money is going instead to the building of the mobile barriers that by 2014 should protect the city from the acque alte and any extreme flooding event.

It looks as though the future for metropolitan Venice no longer lies with the historic city but with the 30 kilometres or so of its waterfront, the stretch of mainland between Porto Marghera and Tessera.

The old industrial zone, now in rapid decline due to the crisis in the Italian chemicals industry, and the airport zone, with all the area in between, are where the new as opposed to historic identity of Venice will be forged. At Marghera there will be a big logistical hub and centre for research and technology. At Tessera, in the so called Quadrante, there will be an airport city, with prestige architect Frank Gehry called in to design the new Porta di Venezia (Venice Gateway). There will be a Las Vegas-style casino, a new stadium, a water terminal and direct connections across the metropolitan area linking up with the imminent high speed train.

A further option is a project that has been under discussion for years: the underwater rail link, the sub-lagunare, that would link Tessera with Venice, stopping at the Arsenale, the historic dockyards of the Serenissima, for which the Comune and central government are trying to devise a new, productive role besides that of housing the Biennale (see Chapter 4, Change of Use). Supporters of the sub-lagunare believe that it would divert some the flow of tourists arriving in Piazzale Roma to that part

(CONTINUED P27)

Rendering of Frank Gehry's design for the Venice Gateway at Tessera, a €800 million project

Deepening the navigation channels is still a risk to the lagoon and therefore also Venice

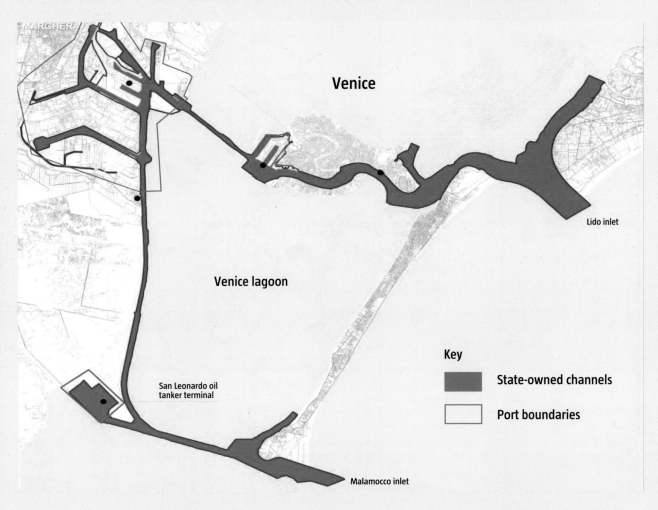

MARGHERA

Venice

Venice lagoon

Lido inlet

San Leonardo oil tanker terminal

Key

State-owned channels

Port boundaries

Malamocco inlet

THE VENETIAN PORT AREAS

On 11 May 2009, Paolo Costa, president of the Venice port authority, presented the public works commission of the Italian Senate with his plan for a major expansion of the goods handling port of Venice, to rival Trieste by making it part of a rail and road hub serving Italy and eastern central Europe. As this requires the entry of very large container ships into the lagoon through the Malamocco entrance to ports at Marghera on the lagoon edge, it will be indispensable to dredge the channels to a depth of minus 12 metres, a process that restarted in 2004 after decades in which it did not take place and is expected to be completed in 2011. The introduction to the submission, with the heading "Environmental protection and the development of the port of Venice", says:

"The dredging of the [navigation] channels and their reclamation, as also the reclamation of 2000 hectares of the port are the precondition of a relaunch of the port of Venice....Now that the situation regarding the lagoon has completely changed and the problem of its hydraulic equilibrium is solved because it will be possible to manage it through judicious use of the Mose system, it is at last possible to describe precisely, and in terms that are respectful of environmental considerations, how the port of Venice will be able to take part in the development of port (and transport) activity in northern Italy, located as it is half way between the African and Asiatic coasts of the Mediterranean and eastern central Europe".

Venice in Peril asked Dr Tom Spencer, director of Cambridge University's Coastal Research Unit, to comment on this statement. (CONTINUED P26)

By Tom Spencer

It is difficult to see how the implementation of the Mose system legitimises the deepening of the navigation channels in the Venice lagoon at the present time.

MOSE is an extreme flood control system but the problems in the lagoon are related to the long-term evolutionary tendency of the lagoon. Previous studies of lagoon bathymetry have been hampered by the difficulty of establishing a datum against which all measurements of lagoon bathymetry and topography can be compared. However, recent advances in field survey methods, and the inter-comparison on surveys through a Geographical Information Systems framework, now allow long-

The Venice lagoon is not a single system but one made up of four sub-basins, each with its own characteristic dynamics

Molinaroli E, Guerzoni S, Sarretta A, Masiol M and Pistolato M 2009. Thirty-year changes (1970 to 2000) in bathymetry and sediment texture
recorded in the Lagoon of Venice sub-basins, Italy. *Marine Geology* 258: 115-25.

Sarretta A, Pillon S, Molinaroli E, Guerzoni S and Fontelan G 2009. *Sediment budget in the Lagoon of Venice, Italy.* Continental Shelf Research
doi: 10.1016/j.cr2009.07.002.

term trends in lagoon bathymetry, morphology and sediment characteristics to be assessed in more detail and with more certainty than has been possible previously.

These studies show a significant deepening of the lagoon and a shift from the complex lagoon morphology of the 1930s to a sediment-starved and subsidence-dominated structure in the 1970s, and from that state to the high-energy and more open, bay-like lagoon of the present day. But these careful studies also show that the Venice lagoon is not a single system but one made up of four sub-basins, each with its own characteristic dynamics.

The largest falls in lagoon bed elevation, reaching 1.2m, have been near the Malamocco inlet and in the Malamocco–Marghera channel. The excavation

of the navigation channels, largely in the 1960s, altered water and sediment circulation patterns in the lagoon. Increased tidal currents and increased wave heights in deeper water have been used to explain the changes in lagoon bathymetry, particularly during strong NE (bora) wind events. These changes have been reflected in the increase in sand contents in bottom sediments, indicating greater tractive forces, and in faunal changes, with bottom dwelling foraminifera (calcium carbonate-shelled organisms in the size range 0.1 to 1-2 mm) typical of 'near marsh' conditions being replaced by species characteristic of 'inner lagoon' environments.

However, detailed studies are still needed to establish the exact nature of water flows in and around the navigation channels and how these processes drive lagoon-floor sediment transport and changes in lagoon-floor morphology.

A proper evaluation of the role of the navigation channels would involve a programme of environmental monitoring at the present time, of sufficient duration (ie; over a number of years) to encompass a wide range of surge and water level conditions and their interaction.

That would need to be followed by a further monitoring period, using identical monitoring protocols, once the Mose system is in operation under the changed water level/surge/water residence time relations that will result from its implementation. Such a before-and-after programme of monitoring would be the only way to rigorously test the assertion made by the Port Authority that "the problem of the hydraulic equilibrium [of the lagoon] is solved". Only then would it be possible to come to an informed decision as to whether or not the navigation channels might be increased in depth.

(CONTINUED FROM P24)

of Venice, the sestiere of Castello, and revitalize it. But this is all highly speculative because there is no definitive design yet for its route or infrastructure, nor a townplanning concept for it in the Comune, nor, indeed, the money to execute it, in all its complexity and with all the risks it may pose for the environment.

But if Marghera and Tessera are the two poles of this new urban system that will have to interrelate with the historic city, the scheme is more the product of isolated proposals or interests than of a real overarching strategy. Not for nothing do the environmentalists inveigh against the millions of cubic metres of cement that would be sunk into the shores of the lagoon at Tessera City, as Enrico Marchi, chairman of SAVE, the company managing Venice's Marco Polo airport, calls the proposed

development around what is already Italy's third largest airport after Rome and Milan.

Tessera City is the plan, not of the Comune, but of Mr Marchi and SAVE together with the Casino (which does, however, belong to the Comune) and they would have majority control of it. For Mr Marchi—whose background is in finance and who is very close to the president of the Region, Giancarlo Galan, a leading member of the Popolo della Libertà party in the Veneto (currently in power nationally) and former director of Prime Minister Silvio Berlusconi's advertising company Publitalia—has for some years controlled the airport company.

This came about because the Region's finance company Veneto Sviluppo, sold nearly all its shares in SAVE to Finanziaria Internazionale Holding SpA, the company controlled by Mr Marchi, thus

PLAN FOR TESSERA CITY
with a second runway for the airport

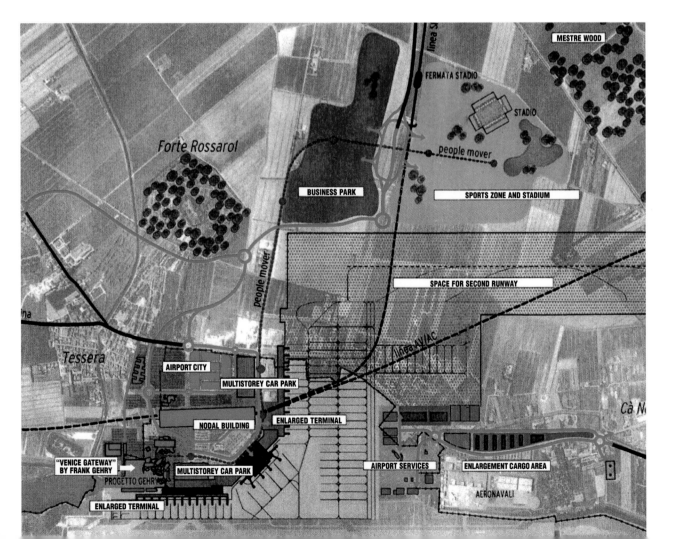

allowing him to become the majority shareholder in the airport, while previously the Region, the Comune and the Province guaranteed public ownership through their shareholdings. They are still shareholders, the Comune (14 per cent), the Province (12 per cent) and the Region (five per cent), but they can no longer impose their will and, indeed, are expected to sell further shares in the near future.

So the way is open for Tessera City, an investment of around €600 million, with another €800 million for the new Venice Gateway by Frank Gehry, the terminal and a second runway. SAVE will be allowed to build another 100,000 cubic metres of office space in exchange for land yielded to the Comune for woods and open space. The Venice Casino, which already has a branch on the mainland at Ca' Noghera, will reopen, much enlarged, at Tessera with an hotel next door, hoping to catch tourists arriving at the airport. The Venice Gateway scheme, with its new water terminal, will also include a large hotel and congress centre.

100m

Euros will be invested before 2012 in developing the Port of Venice to make room for five big cruise ships (currently there is space for three big and one small one)

The former will be 38 metres high, the second, 31. There is a plan to build a 30,000 seat stadium, but with a football team that has just been relegated to D division because it could not afford to pay the championship inscription fee, and without businesses prepared to invest in it, this seems less of a starter.

The future of Porto Marghera also seems uncertain, as everything there turns on the reclamation of severely contaminated ground, poisoned over many years by the petrochemical works. The Comune's masterplan for the area estimates that the reclamation will cost €1.5 billion, without taking into account the cost of building there. This is a sum that the state cannot or does not want to spend and that the private sector will not invest without the likelihood of an economic return.

There is talk now of "semi-reclamation", of adapting to the environment. The lead player in the Marghera project is the new president of the Port Authority, Paolo Costa, predecessor of the present mayor, Massimo Cacciari, and a member of the centre-left Partito Democratico. He enjoys excellent relations with the centre-right, starting with Giancarlo Galan, who supported his appointment.

In the meanwhile, €100 million will be invested before 2011 in developing the Port of Venice to make room for five big cruise ships (currently there is space for three big and one small one). There is no mention of bringing the ships to a port outside Venice rather than taking them through the St Mark's Basin despite repeated requests by the citizens of Venice and the first feeble protests by the Comune because they do not want to deprive the passengers of the thrill of sailing past St Mark's.

The Port Authority is to build a new maritime station on a site between Venice and Mira for ships over 330 metres long that cannot navigate the lagoon.

A terminal for the so-called "sea motorways", will be constructed before 2012 in part of the area once occupied by the Sava steelworks, where cargo and container ships can dock and goods be transferred to rail transport. Construction has already begun in the Vega area for the Science and Technology Park that the Comune launched more than 10 years ago with the universities and other bodies such as ENI, the Italian energy company, the Region and the Province to be an "incubator" for businesses interested in research and innovation. Now, next to Vega 1, there will be Vega 2, Vega 3 and Vega 4, all for service industries, commerce and transport.

Venezia City, which Todini Costruzioni—one of the biggest Italian companies in this sector—want to build here on the edge of the lagoon, would include a 100 metre tall tower with hotels, business centre, parking lot and 44,000 square metres of new buildings.

But for all this territory—there are yet more projects, such as that of Condotte Immobiliare—there are problems relating to land reclamation and lagoon conservation, while adequate urban planning is notable by its absence. In practice, it is private money that proposes and the Comune that bends to its will. In all this pullulating of projects for the terraferma—the Comune, with money of the Fondazione di Venezia, wants to create the Museo di Mestre to give some cultural dignity to the hinterland—the historic city of Venice can only watch.

Instead of being an active participant it seems destined to be the tourist magnet, the showpiece at the centre of the initiatives growing up on its mainland, with it dwindling number of inhabitants mere bystanders.

Chapter 3
Tourism

Anna Somers Cocks
Thierry Morel

- Around 16.5 million tourists a year visit Venice and of these, 12.5 million come just for the day

- A revolutionary new report investigates what would be a sustainable number by calculating safety of circulation. For example, the maximum number of people St Mark's Square can hold is 134,000 a day

- An online information and incentive scheme has been launched to start managing the flow

- Cruise ships are highly profitable and create work in Venice. Their number is due to increase

1
INTRODUCTION

In 1951, 1,128,699 travellers came to Venice; in 2007, it was around 16.5 million.

This chapter deals with what is known about these 16.5 million people: how they got to Venice, where they went when they arrived, and whether their numbers can be managed in the future, rather than allowing the present laissez-faire policy to continue.

The current economic recession notwithstanding, it is hard to see any reason why the number of people wanting to visit Venice should not continue to grow, although at what rate cannot be predicted. The United Nations World Tourism Organisation has forecast that international tourist visits, currently approaching one billion, will reach around 1.6 billion by 2020. Europe will remain the most popular continent to visit and significant increases are expected in tourists from Asia, the Pacific, the Middle East and Africa.

There have been many studies of tourism in Venice, notably one in 1988 which concluded that the ideal daily number of "presences" was 33,000 a day[1]; the main criterion in this case was the optimal number for the maintenance of the tourist industry at the least possible cost to the municipality.

The latest, much more sophisticated report[2], commissioned by the Comune in 2008 from COSES (Consorzio per la Ricerca e Formazione, a research body financed by the Comune and the Provincia of Venice)[2], has a different approach. The emphasis is on the need to manage the flow of tourism and it has been compiled to assist in the development of the new Venice Connected scheme (see page 35). Its objective is to end up with a digital platform capable of giving near real-time information on how full the city is, that will encourage visitors to come in the less crowded periods, offer price incentives and give advice to tour operators of the sort: "Next week, predicted conditions would make it advantageous for you to stay on the Brenta canal and bring people in by the Burchiello boat".

The report has tried to define the conditions for sustainability of access; sustainability of accommodation (hotels, B&Bs etc) both in the historic city and on the mainland; sustainability of circulation (on foot and by water transport); sustainability of cultural activities (capacity of churches, museums and main sites); sustainability of services (rubbish collection, security, medical services etc) and sustainability of use of the city. This last is different for a resident, a commuter, a student or a tourist and the report has only been able to deal with it in a tangential way.

As described in Chapter 1 on Demography, a fundamental concept is that of the "presences" in the historic city; in other words, if you go to Venice and stay there three days, you count as three "presences" for the purposes of the yearly tally and the daily averages. The new report also calculates the "effective population", also taking account of the absences of the residents and non-leisure users of the city, such as students and secondary-home owners, to give an even more precise estimate of the number of people present in the city at any given time. Thus, if you are one of the official residents, you might think you represent 365 presences, but the demographers consider that you go on holiday for two weeks a year, so actually you represent only 350 presences when the daily averages are being calculated. These methodologies are not widely known, which explains why the media often disagree on the total number of tourists.

[1] Costa Paolo and van der Borg Jan, *COSES Informazioni* No. 32/33, 1988

[2] This chapter is much indebted to Scaramuzzi Isabella, Di Monte Giuseppina, Pedenzini Cristiana, Santoro Giovanni, "Turismo Sostenibile a Venezia" *COSES Rapporto* No.141.0, 2009

Less than ideal conditions to see Venice: the Ponte della Paglia, in the background, is one of the most crowded area d.

2

HOW MANY TOURISTS

NUMBERS OF LEISURE VISITORS (PRESENCES + DAY-TRIPPERS) P.A.
By access points to Venice.
Source: COSES, 2008

Basing its conclusions on information supplied by the services that transport people into Venice, the report arrives at 42 million transits a year, equating to 115,000-116,000 people entering or leaving Venice a day.

Of these, in round numbers:
- 8 million p.a. (21,500 a day) are commuters;
- 33 million p.a. are leisure travellers coming and going (therefore 16.5 million arrivals p.a.).

Of these 16.5 million:
- around 4 million p.a. spend at least one night in the municipality of Venice, an average of 9-10 million bed/nights p.a. (25,300 a day);
- 12.5 million p.a. are day-trippers (nearly 34,000 a day).

Conclusion: there were over 21 million tourist "presences" in Venice in 2007 (ie; 9-10 million plus 12.5 million) or slightly over 59,000 "presences" a day (Table 1).

This is already 26,000 more than the 1988 report considered the optimal number of daily presences and is very close to the psychologically important moment when it overtakes the officially resident population of 60,028.

The COSES report points out that most of these numbers are approximate because they are based on information that in some cases is out of date (the last survey of overall numbers entering the city was conducted in 1997, and of commuters, in 2001) and in some cases, does not take account of seasonal variations (eg; in public transport by road). Furthermore, there is the fabled "black economy" of Venice to contend with, and the report duly takes account of this in its estimate of the number of annual bed/nights, because a recent web-based survey[3] shows that there is a 22 per cent discrepancy between the number of rooms-to-rent and B&Bs advertised on the web and the number officially authorized by the Province of Venice.

1. LEISURE VISITORS TO VENICE, 2007
by method of transport.
Source: COSES

METHODS OF TRANSPORT	ARRIVALS	PRESENCES (A)	DAY-TRIPPERS (B) FROM			TOTAL VISITORS (A+B)
			The Lido	Terraferma	Beyond	
Venice & Treviso Airports	1,262,000	3,450,000	-	-	-	3,450,000
Train	509,000	1,347,000	-	450,000	6,667,000	8,467,000
Car	95,000	268,000	-	-	751,000	1,019,000
Tourist Bus	131,000	365,000	-	547,000	1,787,000	2,699,000
Scheduled Bus	44,000	120,000	-	1,110,000	600,00	1,830,000
Cruise Ship	239,000	843,000*	-	-	-	1,278,000
Water Transport	-	-	466,000	160,000	2,235,000	2,861,000
Total Visitors	2,280,000	6,393,000	466,000	2,267,000	12,043,000	21,604,000
Equivalent Population**	6,247	17,515	1,277	6,211	32,995	59,189

*514,000 nights spend on board ** Visitors p.a. divided by 365 days

[3] See *Indagine Strutture Ricettive Extraalberghiere, Indagini sui Siti Web*, July 2008, Comune di Venezia, Assessorato alle Politiche della Residenza

How people get to venice

Unless you have a boat of your own and push off from somewhere on the shoreline of the lagoon, you will be using one of the seven official ways of entering the city, six of them by water and the seventh via the Ponte della Libertà, which connects Venice to the mainland, carrying trains, buses and cars.

By air

Many passengers arriving at Treviso airport, used mostly by Ryanair, are en route to Venice, while this is the case for only slightly over half those arriving at Venice Marco Polo airport, which also serves the whole of the prosperous north east of Italy. The two together account for 1,262,000 tourist arrivals a year; unsurprisingly, they also represent the largest proportion of visitors spending at least one night in Venice.

Air traffic has greatly increased in recent decades, notably through the development of low-cost airlines, and the demand for air travel has brought about a considerable enhancement of infrastructure and services at Venice's Marco Polo Airport, Italy's third largest (by traffic volume) after Rome and Milan.

Marco Polo and Treviso are run by the SAVE group, one of the largest publicly quoted companies in the region, with 1,474 employees (2006). SAVE S.p.A. was incorporated in 1987 and it runs other transport industries and services such as catering and airport shops, the growth of which have made it the largest tourism operator in the Veneto. The company is one of the principal beneficiaries of the growth of tourism and its strategies and policies have a direct impact on the development of tourism in the city (see Cruise ships, pages 44-45, and Chapter 2, Venice on the Mainland). Marco Polo provides links to 148 destinations in 44 countries and has 62 scheduled flights and 76 charter flights per day. The company's revenues in 2008 amounted to €327.6 million (first quarter revenues for 2009 were 13.1 per cent down on the prior year's results for the same period). As such a dominant force in bringing tourists to Venice,

Venice Connected: a first, small step towards managing tourist flows

The closest the Venice municipality has got so far to managing the tourists is a new on-line system that gives them the opportunity to book tickets in advance for services such as public transport, museums and car parking. The scheme, which is called Venice Connected, was launched on 1 February 2009. As well as saving participants' time, it can also save them money as ticket prices depending on their chosen travel dates. Those wishing to come during busy periods will pay more than those who come during quieter seasons.

"Through this system, Venice wants to welcome tourists at its best," explained deputy mayor of Venice, Michele Vianello. "They know in advance if the city is going to be full or not and can save money by planning to come in less crowded periods."

The booking system is available in Italian, English, Spanish, French and German. Clients are assigned a voucher number that guarantees direct access to services in order to avoid queues. Tickets can be booked from seven days in advance.

The first client, Kelly Vilven, a 25-year-old engineer from Seattle was enthusiastic. "I definitely recommend the web site because it is in English and easy to understand and if there are further details needed they get back to you by e-mail right away." Ms Vilven says that, after consulting the scheme's calendar, she chose to visit Venice at a less crowded moment.

According to Mr Vianello, by May there had been around 100,000 visitors to the site, eight per cent of whom made a booking. "This is an extremely satisfactory rate of conversion for e-commerce,"w said the deputy mayor. Customers are already booking as far ahead as November, which is indicated as low season. It is too early to tell if the scheme is making a difference to tourist flows. The most popular purchases have been 72-hour and weekly transport passes, followed by passes for the municipal museum network. "The largest number of customers are French and Belgian followed by the British," observes Mr Vianello, adding that e-commerce is well established in France and Belgium. The council is close to an agreement with the Venice hoteliers' association that would give visitors the chance of booking hotels through Venice Connected. He hopes that major Venice tour operators and the national railway network will also collaborate in future.

[4] Venezia Terminal Passeggeri S.p.A. website, Statistiche

The Venice Arsenale. The Tese della Novissima after restoration.

SAVE's contribution to the revenues of the Comune through taxes, licensing and rents is doubtless significant, but these figures are not publicly available.

By car

Access by car, over the Ponte della Libertà, is limited by the number of spaces in the two parking silos at Piazzale Roma and the one at Tronchetto. Current capacity, assuming two passengers per car, is 22,000 a day, rising to 30,000 in the near future when new parking space will be completed at the Tronchetto.

By train

The station of St Lucia gets by far the largest number of day-trippers, 7,120,000 a year, of which 6,670,000 come from beyond the Comune's

mainland, but are not further defined in the 2009 report. It also brings the second largest group of people to spend at least one night in Venice, 509,000.

By tourist bus

With 2,334,000 a year, this is the second largest group of day-trippers after the train travelers.

By scheduled bus

Not surprisingly, this is the preferred mode of land transport by locals going to Venice for the day, 1.11 million a year.

By water transport

This includes passengers coming to Venice from around the lagoon, but does not include the water connection between the airport and city. This

The vaporetto: not a cash cow

The Azienda del Consorzio Transporti Veneziano (ACTV), founded in 1978, is responsible for running much but not all of the water transport in the city and around the lagoon, as well as bus services on the mainland. It has a fleet of 150 boats, including 52 vaporetti, 56 launches and 10 small launches (with one pilot only) and nine boats for transporting goods and vehicles, and it is also responsible for maintaining 100 pontoons.

In 1998, it created a subsidiary, Ve.La, for developing its commercial and marketing activities under the brand name Hellovenezia. Ve.La now offers other services to tour operators, residents and visitors and it has created online booking facilities for galleries, museums, the performing arts, sport and entertainment.

The vaporetto tickets sold to tourists are much more expensive than those sold to residents but, contrary to popular belief, they do not equate to a lucrative tourist tax

for the Comune. ACTV made a modest profit of €257,829 in 2007 because it has to subsidise loss-making routes such as the ones around the distant lagoon, and the buses on the terraferma.

A single ticket for the vaporetto costs €6.50 for an outsider but €1.10 for a resident who buys a Cartavenezia. This also offers unlimited use of public transport for 12 hours, 48 hours, 72 hours or seven days, as well as all public toilets.

It provides free access to 10 municipal museums, to the 16 churches that are members of the Chorus Association, to the Querini Stampalia Foundation, and the Jewish Museum, and to the casinos in Venice and on the mainland. The number of Cartevenezia sold to tourists in 2007 amounted to €5.3 million. The Carta Venezia for visitors is being supplemented by Venice Connected (see Box, page 34).

category includes the third largest number of day-trippers, 2, 235,000 a year. Curiously, the report assumes that no one arriving by water transport spends the night in Venice.

By cruise ship

The number of cruise ship passengers to arrive in Venice in 2007 was 239,000 a year, who spent an average of nearly nearly four days in town, the longest period for any category of arrival. Visitors also arrive by the big ferries from other countries in the eastern Mediterranean and by hydrofoil and commercial catamaran from the Croatian coast. The huge growth in the port's activities has been in the number of cruise ships, from 200 in 2000 to 510 in 2007. Of the passengers who stay overnight in Venice, 55.5 per cent sleep on board, 15 per cent in three-star hotels, 15 per cent in four-star hotels and 9.4 per cent in five-star hotels[4]. Their spending patterns in the city are shown below (Table 2).

By luxury yacht

Venezia Terminal Passeggeri S.p.A., the company managing Venice's passenger port, is also the majority shareholder in three specialised companies: Venice Yacht Pier S.r.l., founded to develop yachting in Venice; Venice Yachts and Ship Assistance, dedicated to the promotion of services for the large yachts market, and VTP Events s.r.l., created to organize fairs and events.

In fact, as anyone who has been to the opening of the visual arts Biennale in the last few years will have noticed, luxury yachts are more and more a feature of the St Mark's Basin. During 2007, 201 boats tied up, 65 of them longer than 50m and 33 longer than 66m, an increase of 1000 per cent on 2002. They stayed an average of four days, spending between €800 and €2000 a day for various port services, not to mention their expenditure in Venice itself.

Cruise ships to become more frequent

It looks as though the sight of the vast cruise ships will become ever more frequent. Currently, the port of Venice can accommodate three big ships and one smaller one, with three berths for ferries, but by 2012 it will have room for five big ships (250m-315m long) if the plans of the port authority go ahead. The big cruise ships carry a minimum of 2000 passengers, with a maximum of 3,800, rising to 4000 for the new generation.

At present the average stay is 22 hours, so if the berths were constantly occupied, there would be 1,600 moorings a year, with an average of 2000 passengers. In practice, though, this is not the case as the market is strongly concentrated in the months of April through to November. After the port expansion, due to be completed in 2012, the theoretically possible number of moorings would be 1900 p.a., with an average of 2,900 passengers per boat, a total of 15,800 a day. But experience shows that, even if this were to occur, the number of visitors into the city would be reduced by the curious fact that only 60 per cent of the passengers bother to disembark at all.

DURATION OF STAY	AVG. DAILY EXPENDITURE (€)	TOTAL EXPENDITURE (€)
A few hours	19	19
1 night	82	109
2 nights	247	494
More than 2 nights	230	690

2. EXPENDITURE BY PASSENGERS IN EUROS
Source: Centro Ideas, 2006

3
TOURIST ACCOMMODATION IN VENICE

Supply of accommodation of all kinds has significantly increased since 2000, particularly in the B&B category (Table 3), which has almost doubled since 2004 thanks to recent changes in planning regulations that have made it easier for residential property to be transformed into tourist accommodation (see Chapter on Change of Use of Buildings). These tend only nominally to be B&Bs, if one imagines the term to mean a private residence catering for a few guests; instead, they are usually apartments or houses turned over to renting out the rooms and supplying a token breakfast.

Indisputably this has deducted accommodation from the residential stock; the Assessorato alle Politiche della Residenza of the Comune says that 44% of the 952 B&Bs opened 2001-2007— 420 habitations—have been restructured internally so that they are no longer suitable for private occupancy. But because of the number of unofficial enterprises, the number may actually be greater. The profitability of turning your house into a letting business has certainly fuelled the doubling of property prices in Venice since 2000 (see Chapter 4, Change of Use of Buildings) and further encouraged the migration of residents from the historic centre. On the other hand, the benefits are that buildings have been refurbished, thereby improving the fabric of the city, and the visitors in rented flats can mean improved business for local shops and services.

The total number of beds for visitors in the historic centre went up from 28,000 in 2000 to 32,000 in 2004. This represents an increase of 10.9% for the number of hotel beds and 36% for beds in non-hotel accommodation.

Statistics about the tourists who stay in hotels –far easier to measure than those who opt to stay in flats, B&Bs and campsites, or the day-trippers to the city – show, unsurprisingly, that Venice attracts visitors from all over the world.

The USA continues to be the most important country of origin, bigger even than Italy, although the number of American guests in hotels fell between 2006 and 2008 from 460,395 to 366,838 (Table 4).

The figures, although official, need to be treated with some caution. Many observers regard them as underestimates by as much as 30 per cent because of under-reporting by hotels for tax or other reasons. The majority of Venice's hotel guests are Europeans, but this is unsurprising. The United Nations World Tourist Organisation has estimated that 88 per cent of all tourists in Europe are European. Some six per cent are from America, four per cent from Asia and the Pacific, with one per cent each from Africa and the Middle East. European tourists in general, and French and British visitors in particular, tend to stay more nights in Venice. For them, the city may be the main destination for their trip. For non-Europeans making longer journeys, Venice may be one stop on a tour taking in other European cities.

By 2008, 8.5% of all residential buildings in Venice contained B&B accommodation or rooms to rent[5]. The number of furnished flats to rent on short lets has also more than doubled and they represent more than half of all non-hotel type accommodation. The majority of this

[5] *Indagine Strutture Ricettive* op.cit.

3. NON-HOTEL TOURIST ACCOMMODATION IN THE HISTORIC CENTRE
Source: Provincia di Venezia-Settore Turismo, 2008.

TYPE OF ACCOMODATION	2004	2005	2006	2007	2008
Furnished flats	286	308	413	643	768
B&Bs	123	120	129	215	230
Rooms to rent	228	236	200	264	263
Total	637	664	742	1,122	1,261

4. ARRIVALS AND BED NIGHTS IN VENICE BY COUNTRY OF ORIGIN
Source: Comune di Venezia, 2008

COUNTRY	2006 Arrivals	Bed nights	2008 Arrivals	Bed nights
USA	460,395	1,031,127	366,838	864,934
France	188,279	616,368	222,234	668,854
UK	225,226	635,441	211,557	602,240
Total (foreign)	1,764,249	4,657,750	1,790,226	4,894,363
Total (Italy)	265,326	729,945	284,859	782,190
Total	2,029,575	5,387,695	2,075,085	5,676,553

Know your gondolier

- Most common name: Marco, of course
- How many: 425 in the Ente Gondola, with 100 or so reserves, who pay their "principals" 60% of their earnings when allowed to stand in
- Average age: 33
- One woman: Georgia Boscolo, 23, daughter of a gondolier, accepted into the Ente this June
- Fee for 40 minute ride: €150, strictly cash

- Average income: a mystery, but an investigation this year by the Guardia di Finanza discovered that 15 gondoliers who declared an income of €20,000 in 2005 were actually earning €40,000.
- Works hard? Apparently not: even at €40,000 that's less than four hours a week.

LOCATION OF NON-HOTEL TOURIST ACCOMMODATION
Source: Comune di Venezia, Assessorato Politiche della Residenzia, 2008

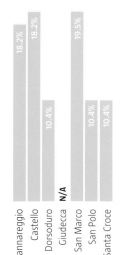

accommodation and 84% of all the B&Bs is in the more central districts (sestieri) of Venice (see graph).

Turning to hotels, the Venetian Hotelkeepers' Association (A.V.A) has 450 members offering 1* to 5* accommodation. Despite obvious limitations on their physical expansion and more rigorously applied planning controls than for B&Bs, rooms to rent and flats, the number of beds offered in hotels is rising steadily to meet tourist demand. Table 5 shows that the number of beds in the historic centre shot up by nearly 30% in just one year.

The year 2007-2008 showed an interesting development: the addition of more luxury accommodation—745 more beds in the five- and four-star category; a sharp decline in the middle range—247 fewer in the three-star category, and a small decline in the cheapest range—120 fewer in

5. HOTEL ACCOMMODATION IN THE CENTRE OF VENICE
Source: Statistics office, Comune di Venezia 2008

TYPE OF ACCOMODATION	2006	2007	DIFFERENCE
Beds	6,982	9,011	+2029
Rooms	3,259	4,053	+794
Baths	2,851	3,936	+1085
Nights	2,234,659	N/A	

the one- and two-star category. All types of non-hotel accommodation, on the other hand, saw an increase in numbers. This may be explained in part by the release in the last few years onto the market of grand buildings, which are now usually allowed to be turned into hotels (see Chapter 4, Change of Use of Buildings), and these have now opened for business.

4

SATURATION POINT

Strada Nuova-Rialto 30,000 people a day Salizzada S.Giovanni Grisostomo

S.Polo-Rialto 15,000 people a day Calle de Mezzo

Rialto-S.Marco 30,000 people a day Ponte de Loro

Rialto-S.Marco 30,000 people a day S.Zulian

Canoniga 15,000 a day

Accademia 15,000 people a day Calle Contarini

Vallaresso 18,000 people a day

S.Zaccaria-S.Marco 90,000 people a day Ponte della Paglia

THE MAIN ROUTES WITH
THEIR BOTTLENECKS
(In red) COSES, 2008

MAIN ROUTES THROUGH
VENICE
COSES, 2008

Venice cannot carry on getting more and more crowded, but how do we estimate when the maximum is reached?

So far as transport is concerned, the 2009 COSES report has modeled its data to produce three scenarios: comfortable, crowded and horribly crowded. Thus, for example, passengers can arrive at Sta Lucia railway station in the following numbers a day: 28,000 (comfortably seated); 42,000 (seated and standing); 65,000 (Mumbai rush hour). The vaporetti down the Grand Canal are comfortable at the rate of 13,000 passengers a day, crowded at 17,000 a day and very disagreeable at 24,000 a day (the number reached if the currently

The maximum of 134,000 people a day in St Mark's Square is close to the 140,000-150,000 that the main routes can carry

most crowded time, 7-9am, is projected over the whole day).

It is reasonable to assume that future policies will aim to avoid at least the third option.

As to how many people can fit into the city, the report has used straightforward arithmetic to arrive at its conclusions. First, it has charted the main pedestrian routes (map page 40) connecting the arrival points in the city (Tronchetto, Marittima, Piazzale Roma, Sta Lucia railway station, San Zaccaria-Cornoldi, the Zattere and the Fondamente Nuove) with the main destinations (the universities, government offices, tourist hot spots, shops). The pulling power of these routes is demonstrated also by the very high concentration of shops along their way.

The four principal routes are:
- Piazzale Roma to Sta Lucia railway station to the Strada Nuova to the Rialto
- Piazzale Roma to the Frari to Campo San Polo to the Rialto
- Piazzale Roma to Campo Sta Margherita to the Calle della Toletta to the Accademia
- San Zaccaria via the Riva degli Schiavoni and the Ponte della Paglia

And from all these to St Mark's Square.

A walking person needs 0.6 m^2, therefore 1.7 people fit into 1 m^2. These routes consist of around 135,000 m^2 of walking surface, so if you divide 1.7m into 135,000 you get a theoretical maximum of 230,000 people—theoretical because people do not march along tidily like guardsmen but dawdle, double back on themselves, sit down on bridges and generally use up more space.

Then the COSES researchers consulted the Polizia Municipale of Venice to find out where the bottlenecks were (aerial view, page 40) and divided them by the modular measurement of a safety exit (0.6 m) to find out how many people could get through them, applying the criteria for outflow from an indoor ground-floor space (a minimum of 50 people) and outdoor space (a maximum of 250).

Assuming therefore a walking speed of 2.5km/h, and outflow capacity of 60 people per module of 0.60 and a time span covering the six peak hour of the day, the maximum number these routes can carry is 140,000-150,000, including people transported down the Grand Canal on vaporetti.

The main objective: St Mark's Square

There is hardly a tourist who does not want to see St Mark's Square, which with the Piazzetta, the Piazzetta dei Leoni and the Molo di San Marco extends over 25,000 m^2, from which you have to deduct 2,000 m^2 covered by cafés such as Florian and Quadri, leaving 23,000 m^2.

On the 1.7 people per m^2 basis, this would allow for 39,000 in the square, but if you think of it as a night club and apply the health-and-safety test to its nine exits, the possible number is reduced to 19,000, with each person occupying 1.2 m^2, and for any length of time, even this is a pretty unattractive prospect. The average stay in the square is 50 minutes; thus, multiplied by the six peak hours and with a turnover index of seven, you get a maximum of 134,000 a day.

Further peak numbers for the area are the Basilica, which can take 14,000 a day, on the basis of 350 people in the church for the current average visit of 10-15 minutes, and the Doge's Palace, with its maximum of 8,000 a day (1.4 million p.a.).

These two are the only museums and/or monuments in the city to have possible problems of overcrowding. The other museums, with the exception of the Accademia, are sparsely attended, most likely because most visitors consider the city itself enough of a cultural experience.

The maximum of 134,000 a day in St Mark's Square is close to the 140,000-150,000 that the main routes can carry, but the public is not the same for both: while most of the tourists in the square will have come down one of these routes, they are also the daily thoroughfares for residents, commuters and students on their way to other objectives.

5
PEAKS AND TROUGHS

Overall, January has the smallest number of tourists and July the highest, but the tourists who sleep in the city are the least seasonal. For them the peak months are July, August, September and October, but even in July, the numbers in hotel and non-hotel accommodation represent only 10 per cent of the annual total sleeping in Venice, while in January, they represent five per cent. In other words, these are tourists who come for the city itself and less for the weather or special festivities such as Carnival.

The 2009 COSES report admits that it needs better data about the day-trippers (47,000-67,000 day), but judging by bus passes and train usage, their season takes off in February with the Carnival, peaks in late April-May with Easter and the 1 May holiday, rises slightly in June, reaches its highest in July, falls sharply in August (which shows that day-trippers prefer not to come to Venice during their summer holidays), flattens out in September and then declines sharply for the rest of the year.

The conclusion is, if you want to avoid crowds it is particularly important not to book when there are feast days, festivals and special events: New Year and Epiphany, Carnival, the opening of the Salone nautico in March, Easter, the national holiday for the Liberation (25 April), 1 May, the Vogalonga and Sensa (May), the opening of the Biennales of visual arts and architecture (especially the former, in alternate years), the Redentore (18 July), the Regata Storica and Film Festival (September), the Immaculate Conception (8 December), and Christmas.

As mentioned earlier, the cruise ships are very seasonal, starting in April, peaking in July, August and September, with a sharp decline from October to zero activity in December, January and early February.

The report then decides how many days a year the various non-leisure city users, both those living in the city and those commuting inwards, are actually present: for example, the 5,937 students living in Venice are deemed to be in town 210 days a year, so in "effective population" terms they count as 3,416 per day. When the local "effective population" per day is added to the tourist "effective population", the total "effective population" of the city is 143, 450.

This is not realistic, of course, as it does not take account of the peaks and troughs. Adjusted seasonally it looks like the graph below, where you can see, for example, that in August the non-leisure users of the city go away, leaving more space for the leisure-users, while September is altogether the worst month for crowding, with both present in force.

THE SEASONAL "EFFECTIVE POPULATION" OF THE HISTORIC CITY
By types of user, 2007

- ● Residents
- ● Second homes
- ● Students
- ○ Commuters
- ○ Tourists
- ○ Day-trippers

Source: COSES, 2008

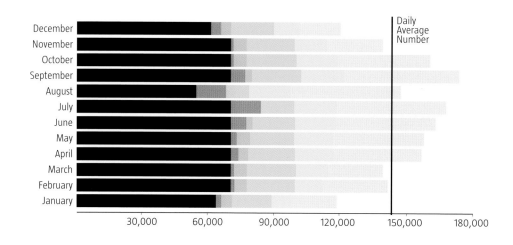

6
CONCLUSION

How many people can Venice hold, comfortably, crowdedly, unpleasantly? If the capacity of transport into Venice is considered together with the capacity of the vaporetti down the Grand Canal and the numbers that can get safely through the bottle-necks on the main routes and fit into St Mark's Square, we have the fundamental elements for making an estimate, when combined with seasonality.

The 2009 COSES report seems reluctant to commit itself. It distinguishes between, on the one hand, tourists who stay in the city and day-trippers from the Comune, and, on the other hand, day-trippers from elsewhere. It stresses that the reason why it does not include these last in its basic assessment of the capacity of Venice is that "they are used as the variable depending on which the logical model establishes the sustainable number".

If the number of over-nighting tourists and day-trippers from within the Comune is added to the residing population (all categories) and the commuters on the "population present" basis—93,000 a day—the Report concludes that Venice can comfortably absorb 26,000 tourists a day (the minimum to keep its tourist economy running), but to this you have to add the average of 34,000 day-trippers from beyond the Comune, so the total becomes 50,000. Bearing in mind that the current average number of tourists a day is 59,000, does this mean that the COSES report already

It is reasonable to assume that visitors from beyond Europe and the USA will become more numerous

considers Venice to be more than comfortably full? It goes on to do further projections, which, puzzlingly, assume a growth in the number of the resident population (unlikely) and commuters, concluding that the absolute maximum, the total saturation point, is 86,000 tourists a day.

The unstated implication of the way the figures are presented, with the day-trippers from beyond the Comune separate, is that this is the category of tourist that most needs management, with the Venice Connected booking system and price incentives as a first step in that direction.

The report concludes by hinting at stronger measures, regretting that only the parking silos and scheduled bus services are under the Comune's authority if it came to limiting inflow, and that an agreement with Trenitalia, the rail system, and Venezia Terminal Passeggeri, the managers of the port, would be desirable.

Cruise ships in Venice: hideous but inevitable?

There is no doubt that sailing into Venice is one of the most glorious sights in the world, but in the case of these cruise ships, should it be allowed, indeed encouraged?

There is widespread dislike in Venice for the cruise ships. In 2006,[1] Mayor Cacciari's Comune tabled a fruitless objection to their sailing into the Bacino di San Marco and progressing down the Giudecca. Local action groups such as Amici di Venezia and the neighbourhood committees have presented petitions and raised questions about air pollution, noise pollution (the ships run their engines constantly) and damage to canal sides from the undertow caused by the moving of so much water as the ship sails by. The Istituto Idrografico noted in 2003 that the gauge installed by St Mark's to register the oscillations of the sea recorded exceptional vibrations on the passing of each of these big ship[2].

In response to these criticisms the Venice port authority had commissioned various surveys on the impact of the traffic. In 2007 the chairman of Venezia Terminal Passeggeri S.p.A , Sandro Trevisano, quoted a first investigation, dating back to 2000: Attilio Adami of Protecno srl concluded that due to their slow speed and the shape of their hulls, the cruise ships caused fewer waves than the vaporetti and lighters. In 2003, Mr Adami addressed the question of the effect of the undertow on the canals opening off the Giudecca and concluded that the action of the water was no stronger than a tide.

This evidence was confirmed, he said, by a study commissioned in 2004 from the Centro Maree (Centre for Study of Tides) and Centro Nazionale di Ricerca (CNR) by the Commissario al Moto Ondoso (Commissioner for Wave Action) of the Comune[3].

Admiral Stefano Vignani, Direttore Marittimo of the Veneto, told the Venice Report that the port authority had obtained the voluntary agreement of the shipping companies to limit the sulphur content of the smoke emitted by the cruise ships entering Venice to 2.5 per cent, now decreasing to 1.5 per cent (the international limit is 4.5 per cent). The Capitaneria of the Port had conducted 50 spot checks over the last year and had found that the limits were very largely being observed.

While more independent research would be desirable, even if it were to show that these ships caused no physical damage whatsoever, the objection to their sailing through Venice would remain because of the aesthetic damage they do: these vast structures with up to 16 decks, more like mega-hotels than sea-going craft, sail into the exquisite detail of the city, obliterating views and making even Sta Maria della Salute look puny.

What is clear, though, is that the cruise market is a highly dynamic sector worldwide and Venice will carry on being a prize destination, with strong economic incentives for the port to keep expanding its activities. The Venice port authority have plans to develop a cruise ship dock for vessels 350m long at the Cassa di Colmata near Fusina, with a shuttle train to bring passengers into Venice railway station, but berthing in the city will obviously remain a great attraction.

The three major operators of cruise ships in the world

The passenger port of Venice is now the 13th largest in the world, and the third biggest in the Mediterranean

are, in order of importance: Carnival, which includes an Italian company Costa; Royal Caribbean Cruise (RCCL), and Star Cruises. Costa operates almost exclusively in the Mediterranean, which makes its ships some of the most regular visitors to Venice. The earlier start of the cruise season, with winter cruises in January and February is primarily responsible for the increase in numbers of passengers, but heavy marketing of fly/cruise holidays also contributed to growth.

The Association of Mediterranean Cruise Ports' 2007 brochure celebrated the increasing success of business in the Mediterranean with the triumphant cry: "Record capacity year-round in 2007". The association has evidently targeted Mediterranean cruises as a big growth area. Ships designed to carry up to 3,500 passengers have been commissioned and since 2004, Carnival has ordered 12 new ships, while RCCL and Star

Cruises have placed orders for three apiece.

There is no doubt about the importance of these cruise ships to the economy of Venice. According to a study carried out by the University of Venice Ca'Foscari Centro IDEAS in collaboration with Risposte Turismosrl[4], direct expenditure by cruise ships accounted in 2007 for €141 million, nearly 10 per cent of the whole Venice tourist economy, estimated by the University of Venice Ca' Foscari's Centro Internazionale di Studi sull Economia Turistica (CISET) to be €1.5 billion a year.

The passenger port of Venice is the now the 13th biggest in the world, after Los Angeles, and the third biggest in the Mediterranean. It is situated in the Marittima, S. Basilio and Sta Marta districts of the historic city and is spread over more than 260,000 m^2, of which the terminals, where the company employs around 1000 people, occupy 44,000 m^2.

It is run by Venezia Terminal Passeggeri S.p.A., founded in 1997 by the Venice Port Authority to manage and develop cruise traffic. It is a mixed public/private sector company whose shareholders include APV Investimenti S.p.A., Finpax S.r.l., SAVE S.p.A., which has a 21 per cent stake in company, promoting fly/cruise holidays operating out of the port of Venice), the Venice Chamber of Commerce and the Comune of Venice.

It is not clear who among this mixed group exerts the greatest influence in decision-making, but it is certainly not the Comune, which does not get much of the profits as it only has a 2.5 per cent shareholding. The economy of the city, on the other hand, benefits as a whole from the employment sustained by the burgeoning port, as well as the from the expenditure by the passengers themselves.

[1] Ordine del Giorno, Comune di Venezia, 22 November 2006

[2] n.a. "Troppe navi, vibrazioni alle stelle", *La Nuova di Venezia e Mestre* newspaper, 6 August 2003

[3] Trevisanato Sandro and Perocchio Roberto, "Il Turismo Crocieristico:u esempio di turismo organizzato, remunerativo e sostenibile" *VeneziaSistemaTurismo* 2007 conference held with VI Commissione Consiliare, Venice 20 November 2007

[4] *L'importanza dela Crocieristica per Venezia: Ricadute socioeconomiche del traffico passeggeri sul territorio*, Centro Ideas, Universitå Ca'Foscari di Venezia, commissioned by the Port of Venice Authority, Venice 2006

Chapter 4
Change of use of buildings

Renato Gibin
Stefania Tonin

- The dwindling resident population and rise in tourism is transforming the economy. The pressure is mounting to change the traditional use of many buildings to cater for the visitors

- There has been an explosion in the number of families turning over their homes to B&B or rented accommodation. In seven years, the figures have risen 1800 per cent and, according to one estimate, 420 homes were thereby lost from the private housing stock

- The value of residential property has more than doubled since 2000

1
INTRODUCTION

THE SESTIERI OF VENICE
The six districts of the historic city

After years of apparent indifference, both experts and the public are taking a strong interest in changes of use affecting buildings in the historic city of Venice. There are heated debates in the press about the spread of B&B establishments (and the loss of ordinary residential accommodation), about projects to convert industrial complexes (such as the former Stucky flour mill on Giudecca and the Arsenale), and about the effectiveness of town-planning and other controls to regulate or prevent this process.

Over the past few decades, the city's economy has gradually lost its traditional variety and complexity, no longer combining manufacturing with a wide range of businesses.

The decline of industry and manufacturing has affected cities everywhere, of course, as they have been replaced by ever more specialised and service-sector businesses. But in Venice, the historic city, the service sector is increasingly focused on tourism. Tourism-related activities have replaced services for businesses and the resident population, and have taken over residential accommodation or vacant industrial premises.

Changes of use in the strict sense have also been compounded by abandonment, under-use and re-use of the building stock on a large scale as a result of demographic changes and by the dynamics of the property market.

Most of the analysis is concerned with the historic city, defined as the districts of Venice 1 (San Marco, Castello, Sant'Elena, Cannaregio) and Venice 2 (Dorsoduro, Santa Croce, San Polo, Giudecca, Saccafisola)

Cannaregio

Castello

Santa Croce

San Polo

San Marco

Dorsoduro

Giudecca

2
CHANGES IN THE ECONOMIC STRUCTURE OF THE HISTORIC CITY

The medium term

Since the end of the Second World War, the economy of the municipality of Venice has undergone a profound transformation. In common with much of Western Europe, there have been two distinct phases: the first from 1945 to the 1970s; the second, from then until the present day.

The first phase was characterised by industrialisation and rapid urbanisation.

- The proportion of the population engaged in agriculture in northern Italy in 1951 stood at 44 per cent but declined to 18 per cent by 1971.
- The proportion of the population employed in industry rose from 29 per cent in 1951 to 39 per cent in 1971.
- The proportion of GNP deriving from agriculture fell from 31 per cent in 1950 to 10 per cent in 1970.
- The proportion of GNP from industry increased from 41 per cent in 1950 to 43 per cent in 1970.

The urban growth was not, however, evenly spread through Italy. Most of the industrial development took place in the north-west, in the Turin-Milan-Genoa triangle, generating an exceptional movement of population from other regions, particularly the south. The changes had a profound effect on the demographics of the country.

- In 1951, 27 per cent of the Italian population lived in the smallest municipalities (those with populations of fewer than 5,000 inhabitants), a proportion which dropped to 22 per cent by 1971.
- The proportion of the population living in medium and large-sized municipalities (in the latter case, the 81 municipalities that in 1951 numbered over 50,000 inhabitants) increased

from 28 per cent in 1951 to 37 per cent in 1971.

The figures are all the more significant when it is considered that the population of Italy increased by 14 per cent between 1951 and 1971.

Trends in Venice during this period were the same as for the other major industrial regions of the north, but the city's economic development was skewed by the growth of large-scale industry at Porto Marghera, on mainland Venice, while the historic city saw the beginnings of demographic and industrial decline.

The second phase of post-war transformation in Italy has been characterised by the expansion of the service sector and by the spreading of industrial and residential settlements.

- In 1981, 51 per cent of all those in employment worked in the service sector. By 2001, the figure had risen to 66 per cent.
- There has been a corresponding increase in the proportion of GNP deriving from the service sector, which first exceeded the 50 per cent threshold in 1981.

Globalisation has also brought about significant changes: we have seen a decline in heavy industry, particularly chemicals, iron and steel, which have relocated to less developed countries, while small and medium-sized enterprises have grown in importance, particularly manufacturing businesses.

DECLINE OF AGRICULTURE
Employment and GNP in different sectors, 1951-1971

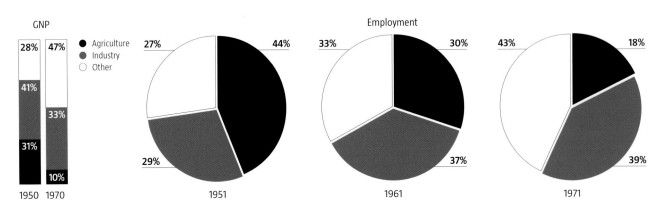

GNP		Agriculture
28%	47%	Industry
41%	33%	Other
31%		
	10%	
1950	1970	

Employment

1951 — 44% / 29% / 27%

1961 — 30% / 37% / 33%

1971 — 18% / 39% / 43%

The 15th-century Scuola Grande of San Marco still houses the the Ospedale Civile

[1] The 2001 statistics take into account only the employees of private businesses, i.e. they do not include public-sector workers.

GROWTH OF THE SERVICE SECTOR
As a proportion of employment in Italy

● Service sector
● All other sectors

This again has led to population shifts, with people and companies moving out of large industrial centres.

The economic role of Venice, a city of large-scale industry in its regional context, has begun to decline: in 1971, businesses located within the municipality, the Comune of Venice (which includes large tracts of the mainland), accounted for 61% of jobs in the province and 12% of those in the Veneto region. Both of these figures had fallen, to 42% and

7% respectively by 2001[1].

The municipality also entered a phase of demographic decline, initially because of net emigration (with most of those leaving moving to outlying municipalities) and subsequently due to the combined effects of migration and a lower birth rate.

The resident population of the municipality declined from a peak of almost 368,000 in 1968 to 270,000 in 2008, a fall of 27 per cent, in 40 years.

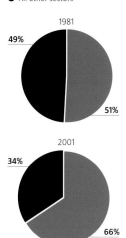

1981

49%

51%

2001

34%

66%

POLARISED URBANISATION
Nationwide distribution of population between different-sized municipalities

● Medium/ large
● Smallest

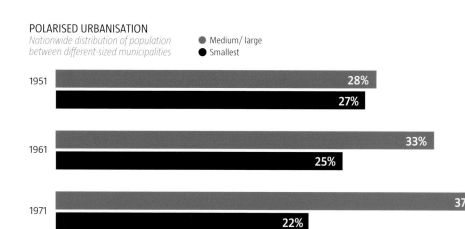

1951   28%
        27%

1961   33%
        25%

1971   37%
        22%

The **only sectors** of economic
activity showing **increases** are
hotels and restaurants, banking,
insurance, and **construction work**

Recent changes in Venice

Against this background, the historic city has followed its own unique course, characterised by two main interconnected phenomena:

- the local economy has shrunk, at least in terms of numbers of jobs, though the decline in employment has not been as severe as the decline in population, partly because of the public-sector jobs connected with Venice's administrative functions;
- there has been an increase in tourism-related private enterprise which has become the great specialisation of the historic city.

These trends are radically transforming the local economy, particularly the private businesses whose

DEMOGRAPHIC DECLINE
Population of municipality of Venice and internal regions

- ● Mainland
- ○ Estuary
- ● Historic city

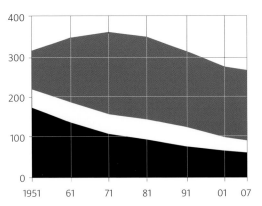

activities are less and less geared to residents and more and more to the needs of those coming into the city to work or as tourists.

The reduction in jobs in the city is connected partly to its demographic decline. The resident population of the historic city has fallen steadily since the Second World War and by 2007 it stood at just over a third of the 1951 figure. Between 1951 and 1971, the change in the distribution of the population was truly striking. While residents in the mainland areas of Venice doubled, the historic city centre lost almost 70,000 inhabitants. Between 1971 and 1991, its population decreased by a further 20,000, and similar numbers were lost in the following 16 years.

With the fall in population, there has been a decline in employment and the causes of both are the same, in part. It is less convenient to house/accommodate people and economic activities in the historic city than elsewhere because of the high cost of transporting people and goods and the high cost of maintaining and modernising premises.

The decline in employment is difficult to illustrate in chronological terms, since the methods used for gathering and recording the statistics has changed over time, so it is not possible to obtain like-for-like data.

Setting aside these difficulties, in particular the fact that the public administration is not adequately represented in the 1971 census, the statistics show a fall in the number of jobs in the historic city by more than 20 per cent from 1981 to 2001.

But the contraction of the economy has been less severe than the decline in the population. We can illustrate this in different ways but it can best be seen in Table 2 (below) showing how employment is distributed in the different parts of the Comune. Since 1971, despite the non-inclusion of public-sector activities in the statistics, the historic city has maintained its proportion of jobs better than its population.

The relatively strong showing of the historic city is due in part to its role as the administrative heart of a much wider area. It has many public and private sector institutions, so many private service businesses find it convenient to locate themselves there.

Between 1991 and 2001, there was an increase, albeit a small one, in the number of jobs in both private and public service activities, the public administration, teaching and health, running counter to the overall negative trend. In the same period, employment in professional activities almost doubled.

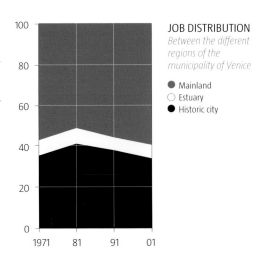

JOB DISTRIBUTION
Between the different regions of the municipality of Venice

- ● Mainland
- ○ Estuary
- ● Historic city

Residential population and visitor numbers

Every day, the historic city is host to people who commute in to work, visit for leisure or tourism, or come to use public and private services. It is not easy to be precise about their numbers but there is no doubt that they are constantly growing and we can make estimates by combining the figures for the different categories of "visitors" (see also the Chapters on Demographics and Tourism).

The size of this daily influx can be roughly gauged by comparing the total number of jobs with the number of residents employed in each sector of the economy. It is an estimate by default, given that it assumes that none of the working residents of the historic city works outside the city, but it is safe to assume that in 2001 the number of people coming in to work, was just under 25,000. Allowing for seasonal and working pattern variations, this is the equivalent to 15,000 resident inhabitants each day.

Young people attending teaching and training institutions also add to Venice's daily "load". The numbers are considerable (the city's two universities have a total of around 25,000 registered students), but impossible to measure using existing sources. The only source available[3] estimates that on any given day, this equates to an extra 4,000 people in the historic city.

Tourist numbers, equally, are anything but easy to measure, but the latest report by COSES (Consorzio per la Ricerca e Formazione) for the Comune (See Tourism Chapter) estimates that there was an average of more than 59,000 tourists a day in Venice. This is almost equal to the officially resident population of 60,028.

[3] Municipality of Venice, Statistics and Research Department. An estimate of the population present in the Municipality of Venice. 2004

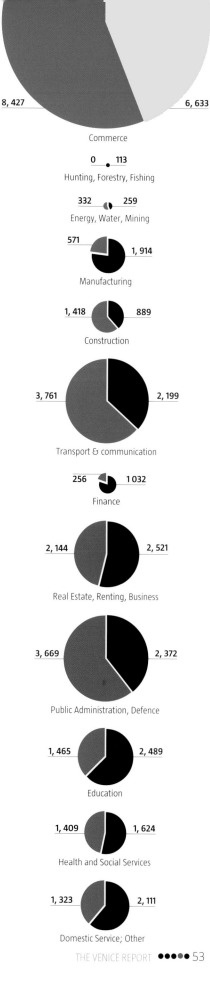

REGULAR INFLUX OF PERSONS
Into the historic city, 2001

⬤ Workers resident in the historic city
⬤ Workers from outside the historic city

8, 427   6, 633
Commerce

0   113
Hunting, Forestry, Fishing

332   259
Energy, Water, Mining

571   1, 914
Manufacturing

1, 418   889
Construction

3, 761   2, 199
Transport & communication

256   1 032
Finance

2, 144   2, 521
Real Estate, Renting, Business

3, 669   2, 372
Public Administration, Defence

1, 465   2, 489
Education

1, 409   1, 624
Health and Social Services

1, 323   2, 111
Domestic Service; Other

The census districts around **St Mark's Square** and on the route into the city centre from the **Ponte della Libertà** are the most **geared to tourism**

Hotels, bars and restaurants: an economy geared to non-residents

The local economy has recently come to specialise in providing services for people who use the city but are not resident. The only employment sectors that showed increases between 1991 and 2001 were professional services and the hotel, bar and restaurant trades. Moreover, in 2001 the latter became the most important private-sector activity for jobs.

The trend is confirmed by a more recent source (ASIA, the Italian Statistical Business Register), concerned with private sector jobs, demonstrating that the only sectors of economic activity showing increases in Venice are hotels and restaurants, banking and insurance, and construction work.

The degree of specialisation of the economy of the historic city is summed up in a single figure: 30 per cent of all private sector employment (excluding fishing, hunting, education and health) depends on hotels and restaurants.

Hotels, bars and restaurants are spread throughout Venice, and in some thoroughfares and areas this type of business is predominant. The following maps illustrate the degree of tourist-dependant specialisation of the different census districts of the centre, showing the percentage of jobs in tourism in relation to employment as a whole.

The maps show that:
● the density of hotels, bars and restaurants varies considerably from one area to another;
● some districts are highly specialised (true in both 1991 and 2001), with almost all employment accounted for by hotels, bars and restaurants;
● the number of census districts registering a

high degree of specialisation increased between 1991 and 2001;
● the census districts around St Mark's Square and on the route into the city from the Ponte della Libertà (the bridge linking Venice with the mainland) are the most geared to tourism (true in both 1991 and 2001);
● between 1991 and 2001, the areas of high specialisation spread out in almost all directions from San Marco and the thoroughfare leading into Venice.

The maps do not, of course, convey the complete picture. Many other services operate at least in part for the non-resident population. The most obvious example is transport: those working in this sector not only transport non-residents, but also move the goods used for tourism-related activities and for the economic activities in which non-residents are involved.

We have tried to make a rough estimate of the contribution of activities other than hotels and catering to the "non-resident economy". Here, we propose two models: a narrow definition, referred to for the sake of simplicity as the "tourism economy model", which identifies the "non-resident" economy as consisting of activities

NUMBER OF EMPLOYEES
Percentage change in each sector, 1991-2005

● Historic city 2001-2005
● Municipality 2001-2005
○ (Historic city 1991-2001)

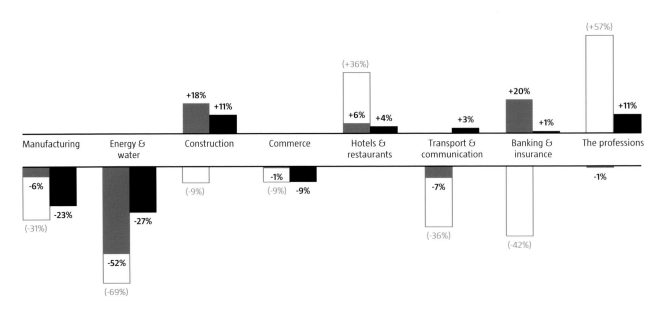

Manufacturing	Energy & water	Construction	Commerce	Hotels & restaurants	Transport & communication	Banking & insurance	The professions
-6% / -23% / (-31%)	-52% / -27% / (-69%)	+18% / +11% / (-9%)	-1% / -9% / (-9%)	(+36%) / +6% / +4%	+3% / -7% / (-36%)	+20% / +1% / (-42%)	(+57%) / +11% / -1%

JOBS IN HOTELS, BARS AND RESTAURANTS

In different census districts in 1991 (above) and 2001 (below)

- ● Between 40 and 70%
- ● Over 70%

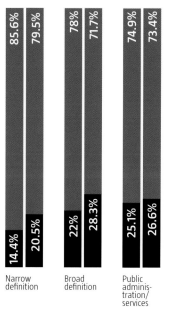

JOBS IN THE NON-RESIDENT ECONOMY

In the historic city, 1991 to 2001

- ● "Non-resident" economy
- ● Other jobs

	Narrow definition	Broad definition	Public administration/ services
Non-resident (top)	85.6% / 79.5%	78% / 71.7%	74.9% / 73.4%
Other jobs (bottom)	14.4% / 20.5%	22% / 28.3%	25.1% / 26.6%

geared principally to non-residents, and a broad model, which takes into account services for both populations.

In practical terms, the narrow model defines hotels, restaurants, bars, non-shop-based retailing, glass manufacture, camp sites, short-stay accommodation, refectories, canteens, cafeterias, travel and tourism agencies and other tourist assistance services as belonging to the non-resident economy.

The broad model covers jobs in manufacturing, production and distribution of gas, electricity and water, waste disposal, non-specialised retailing, retailing of foodstuffs, beverages and tobacco, pharmaceuticals, medicines, cosmetics, perfumes, maritime, coastal and inland waterway transport, scheduled and non-scheduled air transport, handling of goods and warehousing and other transport.

The broad model is based on the assumption, discussed earlier, that the non-resident population is virtually equal in number to the resident population, and that some services and jobs owe their existence and provide services equally to both groups.

Our broad definition attributes to the "non-resident" economy the jobs contained in the narrow model plus half of the jobs associated with transport, certain categories of retail commerce, the supply of electricity, water and gas, and waste management.

This is still a conservative definition because it does not include other activities, such as construction, which undoubtedly benefits, and is helped by, the non-resident population.

Analysing the two models, it is clear that the economy of the historic city is increasingly specialising in favour of the non-resident population:

- ● in 1991, the "non-resident" economy accounted for 14 per cent of jobs, according to the narrow definition, and 22 per cent by the broad definition;
- ● by 2001, the figures had increased to 20 per cent and 28 per cent respectively.

It is also worth pointing out that by 2001, the "non-resident" economy, as broadly defined, provided more jobs than public administration and public services.

Using the ASIA database, the trend is even more marked. By 2005, 33.3% of "narrow definition" and 47.6% of "broad definition" sector jobs in the private sector in the centre depended on the "non-resident" economy.

The Arsenale: a 50-year stalemate over its change of use

As in the Arsenal of the Venetians
Boils in the winter the tenacious pitch
To smear their unsound vessels o'er again,
For sail they cannot; and instead thereof
One makes his vessel new, and one recaulks
The ribs of that which many a voyage has made;
One hammers at the prow, one at the stern,
This one makes oars, and that one cordage twists,
Another mends the mainsail and the mizzen...

From Dante's Inferno, translated by Longfellow

By Lidia Panzeri

The first famous reference to the Venice Arsenale is by Dante, who describes the frenetic activity of the place even in winter. When he was writing, in the early 14th century, the original 12th-century yard had already been enlarged with the creation of the Arsenale or Darsena Nuova (new dock or basin). Between 1473 and 1573, there was further substantial enlargement, with the creation of the Arsenale Novissimo, the construction of the Gaggiandre by Sansovino, and the addition of the Darsena delle Galeazze.

Venice's sea power was at its height, due in part to its shipyards, which anticipated modern industrial methods by several centuries: from the design, jealously protected by very strict laws, to the launch of a ship, every area was devoted to a specific activity. Whether making ropes or designing weapons, each department worked independently, until the final assembly stage.

The result was that, at the time of the Battle of Lepanto against the Turks in 1571, the Arsenale could turn out a galley – the most typical of the Republic's ships, with an optimal relationship between loading capacity and agility of manoeuvre – in just one week.

The Arsenale continued to expand in the following centuries. In the mid-1700s, the Squadratori building, where ships' main timbers were laid down, was erected facing the Darsena delle Galeazze. Then, between 1872 and 1915, dry-dock facilities were created in the northern part of the complex. The final building works were undertaken in 1916, consisting of accommodation for naval personnel.

The Arsenal was still active during the Second World War, when it employed 5,000 workers, but it was eventually closed down in 1957, when the Command Centre of the Maritime Department of the Upper Adriatic was transferred to Ancona.

This was a severe blow to the city, particularly the Castello district, where most of the skilled workers, or "arsenalotti", lived. It also marked the beginning of the physical deterioration of the buildings, many of which are in danger of collapse, or have collapsed already.

Dimensions and ownership

The Arsenale covers 48 hectares on the north-eastern edge of the city, accounting for one fifteenth of the total area of the historic city (700 hectares). It is worth noting that the surrounding wall, five kilometres in length, was not intended to defend the city, already protected by the lagoon's defence system, but to safeguard the shipbuilders' secrets.

The Ministry of Defence / Navy owns 296,161 square metres (62%), located mainly on the southern part of the site.

The Ministry for Infrastructure and Transport owns 9,350 square metres (2%).

A further 172,489 square metres (36%) is state property, under the control of the Soprintendenza per i Beni Architettonici e per il Paesaggio, the government officials responsible for architectural heritage and landscape.

Restoration

According to a reliable, though not particularly detailed, estimate, it would cost €503 million to rehabilitate the entire Arsenal complex completely (roughly one-tenth of the cost of the MOSE, the city's flood defence system). This sum breaks down as follows: €381 million to rehabilitate and restore the buildings and €122 million to bring mains services up to standard and rebuild the paving and embankments.

The agencies most active in this area are the Venice Soprintendenza per i Beni Architettonici e per il Paesaggio and the Magistrato delle Acque (a peripheral agency of the Ministry for Infrastructure and Transport). But the Soprintendenza has a supervisory role in all restoration work.

The first – state funded – interventions were carried out in 1983, to restore the Corderie (old rope-making workshops). Subsequently work has been done on the Gaggiandre dock, the Artiglierie (armoury), the Isolotto (small island) and the Tese delle Vergini (a long rectangular warehouse building), all of which are used for the Biennale and cover a total area of 20,000 square metres on the southern part of the site.

The Arsenal's monumental entrance gate on the landward side has also been restored.

The Magistrato delle Acque, meanwhile, has worked mainly on the northern part of the site. In 2001 and 2002, in conjunction with the IUAV (Venice University Institute for Architecture), a survey of the whole five kilometres of surrounding wall was carried out, and the

Ferrovia

Fdm Nuove

Rialto

Accademia

San Marco

San Giorgio

Sant'Elen

Giudecca

© Insula Spa

Location of the Venice Arsenale dockyard

most dilapidated sections were subsequently restored. Several buildings in danger of collapse were made safe, in the areas of the Galeazze and the Tese Novissime.

The embankments in this area were also restored and made safe.

Venice in Peril has adopted the restoration of the 1883 Armstrong-Mitchell crane, the only surviving example of seven exported to ports around the world.

Numerous stakeholders and little investment

Debate over the future of the Arsenal has been going on for nearly half a century. At present, however, interest has died down and the recommissioning of the area no longer seems to be a priority for the current municipal council, led by Mayor Massimo Cacciari. This, together with changing of the guard at both the Magistrato delle Acque and the Agenzia del Demanio (State Property Office), two key stakeholders, has resulted in a stalemate where redevelopment of the Arsenal is concerned. A change in Ministry of Defence has resulted in new thinking regarding the area belonging to the Italian Navy.

Nevertheless, plans are taking shape, especially where the northern part of the Arsenal complex is concerned. A key factor has been the creation of Arsenale S.p.A., a company in which the State Property Office holds 51% of the shares, the Municipality of Venice 49%. Operating since 2005, its chairman is Roberto d'Agostino, who served three terms as head of the municipal town planning department and was responsible for the rehabilitation of the Giudecca, as well as promoting plans for the new bridge over the Grand Canal by star architect Santiago Calatrava.

There have been three stages in the planning of the Arsenal re-development: the 1998 Programme for urban rehabilitation and sustainable development of the territory (PRUSST), which set the issue in the wider context of the development plan for the city of Venice (piano regolatore); the executive document (documento direttore), approved by the Municipal Council in February 2001, which set out more specific objectives for the area; and finally the detailed PP8 North plan, approved by the Municipal Council on 25 March 2003, which focuses on the northern part of the complex. Oddly, there is no plan at all for the waters of the Arsenale, not even to house historic Venetian boats that have been lovingly restored by associations of local enthusiasts.

Northern area

Apart from the submariners' barracks area, the northern part of the site belongs to the civil department of the State Property Office. It includes the dry docks, which have been leased partly to the ACTV, which uses them for repairing its vaporetti (water buses), partly to the Consorzio Venezia Nuova, which will be using them for maintaining the MOSE flood defence system. The remainder comprises the Tese Nuovissime (tese is Venetian term for factory sheds or warehouses), some barrack-type accommodation and the Porta Nuova (new gate).

The very first stage in the transformation of this area was undertaken in 1998 by Thetis S.p.A., a marine technology research company, which restored three buildings in danger of collapse for its own use.

The plans for this area also envisage the establishment, by 2010, of the offices of the Consorzio Venezia Nuova and the CNR (National Research Centre), and at a later stage those of the Fondazione dei Musei (Museums' Foundation). Another building will be

The last surviving Armstrong-Mitchell crane of 1883 is in the Arsenale

The Arsenale's 48 hectares represent one-fifteenth of the city's total area, so its future could play a major role in the future of Venice

used to house a laboratory for restoring contemporary art videos and installations. Sheds (tese) 105 and 113, for which plans have already been drawn up, will house catering services.

Beyond the Tese Nuovissime stands the Porta Nuova, a tower which will be used as an exhibition centre. Restoration work is due to start there in the very near future). It is envisaged that this tower will in future be linked by a moveable bridge (for which the plans already exist) to the Gaggiandre, in the southern part of the site, making it possible to move freely around the whole Arsenal complex.

Southern area

The southern part of the site belonging to the Ministry of Defence and the Navy retained its military functions until the recent war in Kosovo.

This area above all preserves the memories of the naval feats of the Serenissima (Venetian Republic) and the Austrian and Italian regimes that followed it. Of this glorious past, there remains for the time being one

solitary witness, the submarine Dandolo, which saw service in the Second World War

There are ambitions to create a museum that would preserve the centuries-old history of the area, but the project has had to be suspended because, when the invitation to tender was issued last December (2008), no partner was found to co-fund the venture.

There is, however, a project – also awaiting funding – to convert the former Squadratori building into a headquarters for the Institute of Naval Studies (Istituto di Studi Marittimi Militari), which would also house all the Biblioteca Marciana's books on naval topics (see photograph).

A large part of this area, beginning with the Corderie, has been used by the Biennale to stage its art, architecture, music and dance activities. The Biennale would like to occupy these buildings permanently, once the problem of heating them has been solved. The Biennale's agreement with the Navy dates from 2000 and has been renewed several times.

When everything is up and running, the various activities should provide jobs for some 3,000 people, almost as many as in the past. The present figure is around 300, excluding seasonal staff employed by the Biennale.

The main difference is that most of the people concerned will be researchers rather than the skilled workers and craftsmen who played such an important role in the success of the Arsenale, the Serenissima's great shipyard.

3
IMPACT OF CHANGE: PROPERTY VALUES IN THE HISTORIC CITY

The development of the economy geared to "visitors" has led to changes in the use of buildings with new activities replacing former businesses, taking over residential property or occupying unused buildings.

These changes have been governed by property prices, the Venice property market being particularly lively.

Italian property prices have risen in recent years, with residential prices increasing between 2000 and 2006, despite a minor fall in 2001 because of the abolition of the INVIM tax[*]. There was also a drop in 2007. The cost of office premises across the country has increased on average by 46 per cent since 2000, while the commercial premises sector has been the most stable, with the least overall growth.

In Venice, there have been average annual increases of 11.21 per cent in the price of residential property, 5.84 per cent for office premises and 6.70 per cent for commercial premises such as shops since the year 2000.

[*]INVIM (tax on the increase in value of real estate) was abolished in January 2002, sooner than planned. This resulted in property sales/purchases, or at least the registration of such sales/purchases, being held over from 2001 to 2002

AVERAGE PROPERTY VALUES
In the historic city of Venice, 2001 - 2008

YEAR	PROPERTY TYPES					
	Residential property (average weighted values in euro)	Residential property index (year 2000 = 100)	Offices (average weighted values in euro)	Office premises index (year 2000 = 100)	Shops (average weighted values in euro)	Commercial premises index (year 2000 = 100)
2000	2, 296	100	2, 714	100	3, 987	100
2001	2, 408	105	2, 834	104	4, 251	107
2002	3, 470	151	3, 078	113	4, 918	123
2003	3, 779	165	3, 309	122	5, 291	133
2004	4, 164	181	3, 567	131	5, 709	143
2005	4, 430	193	3, 808	140	6, 065	152
2006	4, 769	208	4, 020	148	6, 498	163
2007	4, 070	177	4, 263	157	6, 656	167
2008	4, 497	217	4, 265	157	6, 656	167

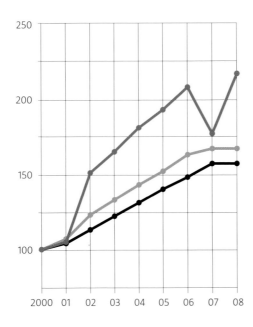

AVERAGE PROPERTY VALUES
In the historic city of Venice, 2000, 2008

- ● Residential property
- ● Office premises
- ● Commcercial premises

The table to the left sets out average values in euros for each type of property in the city for the years 2000-2008 using data provided by NOMISMA, a property market index, which publishes surveys of the principal areas of Italy. The valuations are weighted averages, taking into account market values as they differ from one area to another. For residential property, this means prestige areas, semi-central areas, outlying areas etc. Offices and shops are valued according to whether they are located centrally, semi-centrally, or on the outskirts.

It can be seen that the value of residential property has more than doubled since 2000. The largest increase, of 45 per cent, was in the period 2001–2002, probably reflecting the introduction of the single European currency.

4

THE EFFECTS OF THE CHANGES: HOW THE BUILDING STOCK IS BEING USED

Economic and demographic developments have over time changed the ways in which the building stock is used. The principal changes have been an increase in the proportion of residential dwellings used by non-residents (who may use the accommodation for work, study or as a secondary home) and an increase in the proportion of buildings used for tourism-related activities.

The available sources do not enable us to build up a complete picture of the ways in which the building stock is used. In particular, we lack reliable information regarding use of non-residential buildings. It is, however, possible to analyse the various trends separately, using different sources. The topic is nonetheless difficult to deal with, and we must first establish some definitions.

Normally, the term "change of use" refers to a town-planning procedure that takes the following course:

- the city development plan registers or prescribes the type of use made of every building (or area) and specifies, on the basis of the characteristics of the areas concerned, what alternative uses are permitted;
- when the owner of a building wants to use it for a different purpose, he applies to the relevant department of the municipal administration for authorisation to do so;
- having checked whether the application is admissible in terms of the city development plan, the administration grants (or refuses) permission;

- permission for a change of use must be granted before the owner can obtain the further permits he will need in order for the activities he has in mind (e.g. permits issued by the health authorities).

Finally, the effective use of the building is registered with the land registry (catasto). This administrative register is managed by the Agenzia del Territorio (Spatial Planning Agency), a public body dependant on the Ministry for the Economy and Finance.

Changes of use would be relatively easy to measure if the administrative departments concerned registered them and made the information available, but for many changes of use related to the non-resident economy it is not necessary to follow town-planning procedures. This is the case when:

- a residential building is converted into a non-hotel-type facility for visitors (ie B&B or rooms to rent);
- premises used for commercial or small-scale-industrial/craft activities for the resident population are converted for similar activities for the non-resident population.

Changes of use

* The catasto was, until recently, regarded as the worst of public administrative registers (not up-dated and inaccessible), a stigma that the work of updating of recent years has not entirely removed. Only recently has the Agenzia del Territorio, (which manages the register), begun to open itself up by publishing statistics, or allowing access to it at low cost.

Some information can be obtained from the administration, particularly in the more structured part of the economy – for example, when hotels take over buildings previously devoted to residential or other uses.

The land register (catasto*) is a source that has not been much used until recently for our type of analysis. It obviously records changes that have taken place in line with the regulations but changes of use may also have occurred without authorisation, and are therefore not registered. Illegal changes of use under town planning requirements are, however, probably more limited in number than other less regulated forms of change.

The land registry lists and describes the properties concerned (the structures and their dimensions), recording their location and boundaries, the persons claiming rights (of various kinds) over them, and the rateable value of the property (rendita catastale). The catasto, as we now have it, was instituted in the early years of the 20th century and consists of two different registers, one for urban buildings, the other for landed property. It has become increasingly important in recent years because rateable values as assessed by the land registry are used for calculating the municipal

There have been **annual price increases** of **11.21 per cent** for residential property, **5.84 per cent** for offices and **6.70 per cent** for shops since 2000

PROPERTY TYPES
Land register categories. Source: Interdepartmental Finance and Budget Department of the Comune of Venice

CATEGORY		TYPE
A00	Other dwellings	A - units for residential use
A01	Aristocratic/patrician dwellings	A - units for residential use
A02	Middle-class dwellings	A - units for residential use
A03	Lower-middle-class dwellings	A - units for residential use
A04	Working-class dwellings	A - units for residential use
A05	Lower-working-class dwellings	A - units for residential use
A06	Rural dwellings	A - units for residential use
A07	Small detached dwellings	A - units for residential use
A08	Villas	A - units for residential use
A09	Castles, palaces of artistic and historical importance	A - units for residential use
A10	Offices and private studios	A - offices and private studios
A11	Dwellings and lodgings typical of the place concerned	A - dwellings and lodgings typical of the place
B00	Other communal buildings	B - communal buildings
B01	Colleges, boarding schools, places of education, orphanages, hospices, convents, seminaries, barracks	B - communal buildings
B02	Not-for-profit care homes and hospitals	B - communal buildings
B03	Prisons and reformatories	B - communal buildings
B04	Public offices	B - public buildings
B05	Schools and scientific laboratories	B - public buildings
B06	Not-for-profit recreational and cultural centres, not housed in buildings in category A/9	B - public buildings
B07	Chapels and oratories not used for public worship	B - communal buildings
B08	Underground warehouses for storing provisions	B - warehouses
B10	Other communal buildings	B - communal buildings
C00	Other buildings used for commercial or small-scale industrial activities	C - other (commercial/small-scale industrial)
C01	Shops	C - shops
C02	Warehouses and depositories, cellars and lofts if not adjoined to a dwelling unit	C - warehouses and depositories
C03	Art and crafts workshops	C - art and crafts workshops
C04	Buildings and premises for sporting activities	C - units for sports and bathing/swimming
C05	Bathing and spa establishments	C - units for sports and bathing/swimming
C06	Cattle sheds, stables, depots and garages	C - hangars, garages, car parking
C07	Hangars, private car parking spaces, covered car parking	C - hangars, garages, car parking
C10	Other buildings for commercial or production activities	C - shops
D01	Factories	D - factories
D02	Hotels and boarding houses	D - hotels and boarding houses
D03	Theatres, cinemas, concert and entertainment halls, arenas, playgrounds, zoos/safari parks	D - theatres, concert halls, cinemas
D04	Care homes and hospitals	D - communal buildings
D05	Banks and insurance institutions	D - Banks
D06	Buildings, premises, areas equipped for sporting activities	D - other cultural and sporting facilities
D07	Buildings for industrial activity, which could not be used for other purposes without a radical conversion	D - industrial buildings
D08	Buildings for commercial activity, which could not be used for other purposes without a radical conversion	D - commercial buildings
D09	Structures which float or are secured to a fixed point, private toll bridges, areas for mooring balloons and airships	D - other buildings
D10	Buildings for agriculture-related production activities	D buildings for industrial activities (agri-culture)
E01	Stations for land, maritime and air transport services, underground train stations, railway stations, ski-lifts	
E02	Municipal and provincial toll bridges	E - other buildings
E03	Structures and buildings for special public requirements	E - other buildings
E04	Enclosed facilities for markets, trade fairs, cattle markets and similar	E - other buildings
E05	Fortifications and their outbuildings	E - other buildings
E06	Light houses, semaphore stations, towers for making use of the municipal clock	E - other buildings
E07	Buildings used for public worship	E - other buildings
E08	Buildings and structures in cemeteries, excluding burial niches, tombs and family vaults.	E - other buildings
E09	Buildings for special uses not included in the group E categories above	E - other buildings
F01	Urban space	F - other
F02	Derelict units	F - other
F03	Units under construction	F - other
F04	Units in course of definition	F - other
F05	Sun terrace/flat roof	F - other

[2] This is true of illegal non-hotel-type accommodation. A recent survey of websites publicising non-hotel-type facilities in the historic centre revealed that at least 20% of those advertising their services were not recorded in the mandatory public registers.

[3] This information, not usually available in such detail, was provided by the Interdepartmental Finance and Budget Department of the Municipality of Venice.

property tax, which has become the main source of income for Italian municipalities.

For our analysis, we have studied the number of property units, the sum of their sizes, their categorisation and their location, as recorded in the new urban buildings register, first on 31 December 2000, then on 30 June 2008.

The information relates to individual property units, a unit being a portion of a building, an entire building, a group of buildings or an area "which, in its present state and according to local use, has the potential for autonomy in terms of function and income generation".

Property units are classed in categories. There are more than 50 such categories but, to attempt simplicity, we have reclassified them under 25 different headings.

Given the definition of a property unit, simply comparing numbers is not, of itself, useful in measuring changes of use. This is because a change in the number of units might be the result of one unit being split into two or more, or pre-existing units being combined, rather than a real increase in the number of units.

THE SESTIERI OF VENICE
The six districts of the historic city

NUMBER OF PROPERTY UNITS
Recorded in the catasto (Building Registry), 2001 to 2008

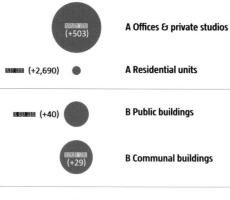

For this reason, we have used an additional piece of information, which comes under the heading "consistenza" (size). This is currently available only for register categories A, B and C, and is defined differently for each category. In the case of category A units, size is expressed in terms of the number of "useful" rooms plus, on a proportional basis, the number of accessory rooms.

A "useful" room is a one serving a principal function (bedroom, living-room, kitchen etc.), having its own source of daylight and a floor area of at least eight square metres. For category B units, size is expressed in cubic metres. The volume is calculated on an "all-in" basis, from pavement level to the intrados of the last habitable storey. For category C units, size is measured in square metres, taking into account the surface area of the principal rooms used for commercial purposes and including a proportion of the area of accessory rooms.

We have measured changes of use by comparing the classification of property units at December 2000 and June 2008. But comparison is complicated by uncertainties about the quality of the database on the two different dates. A new digital version of the 2000 register contains a large number of property units for which the information is incomplete.

As the tables on the following pages demonstrate, both the number and size (consistenza) of property units in the city centre increased between the two dates.

The number of units increased by six per cent overall, but the percentage increases varied considerably from category to category:
- the number of category A (residential) and category C units (commercial/ small-scale industrial) increased by eight per cent and nine per cent respectively, close to the general average;
- the numbers of units in categories D (commercial buildings including hotels, boarding houses, banks and insurance institutions) and B (public and cultural buildings) rose by 30 per cent and 21 per cent respectively, much higher than the average;
- in category A, there was a large increase in the

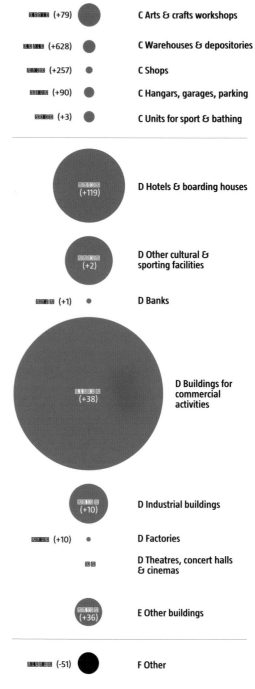

A Offices & private studios (+503)

A Residential units (+2,690)

B Public buildings (+40)

B Communal buildings (+29)

C Arts & crafts workshops (+79)

C Warehouses & depositories (+628)

C Shops (+257)

C Hangars, garages, parking (+90)

C Units for sport & bathing (+3)

D Hotels & boarding houses (+119)

D Other cultural & sporting facilities (+2)

D Banks (+1)

D Buildings for commercial activities (+38)

D Industrial buildings (+10)

D Factories (+10)

D Theatres, concert halls & cinemas

E Other buildings (+36)

F Other (-51)

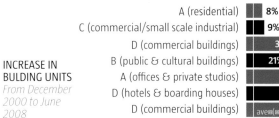

A (residential)	8%
C (commercial/small scale industrial)	9%
D (commercial buildings)	30%
B (public & cultural buildings)	21%
A (offices & private studios)	40%
D (hotels & boarding houses)	57%
D (commercial buildings)	ave﹍(﹍﹍) 130%

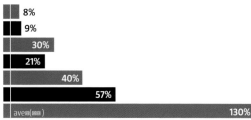

"offices and private studios" class (40 per cent);

• in category D, there was a large increase in "hotels and boarding houses" (57 per cent) and an even larger increase in buildings used for commercial purposes (130 per cent).

The geographical distribution of the changes was also very uneven:

• the number of category A units increased by 17 per cent in Giudecca district, but by only five per cent in Sant'Elena and one per cent in Santa Croce;

• of the category A units, those classed as "offices and private studios" increased by over 50 per cent in the districts of Castello, Dorsoduro and San Polo;

• units in the "hotels and boarding houses" class increased by less than 50 per cent in the districts of Cannaregio, Dorsoduro and San Polo, while a third of all units in this category were in the San Marco district;

• units classified as "commercial buildings" increased by over 200 per cent in the Santa Croce district, which already accounted for a third of the buildings of this type in the historic city.

The information using size (consistenza) provides evidence of less rapid growth, a sign that a sizeable proportion of the increase in units may well have been due to the splitting up of pre-existing ones.

The changes that occurred between 2000 and 2008 nevertheless reflect increases across the board:

• in category A properties, the total number of rooms increased by seven per cent;

• in category B properties, the cubic metre figure increased by six per cent;

• in category C properties, the square metre figure increased by one per cent.

The percentage increases were nevertheless very unevenly distributed, in terms of both category and locality:

• in category A, the overall number of rooms in residential units increased by six per cent, but for offices and private studios it went up by 45 per cent;

• only in the districts of Cannaregio and San Marco did the number of rooms in offices and private studios increase by less than 50 per cent;

• the percentage increase in the number of rooms in residential units was broadly similar from one area to another, with the exception of Giudecca (+15 per cent) and Santa Croce (no change);

• the cubic metre figure for category B properties increased by 31 per cent in Cannaregio, but fell by 15 per cent in Castello;

• changes in the square metre figure for category C properties varied from +14 per cent in San Marco district to -11 per cent in Giudecca.

Simplifying considerably, we cannot maintain that the increase in the number of property units used as hotels and restaurants, though considerable over the period 2000-2008, has greatly reduced the proportion of residential accommodation. This is not the case, however, with the growth in non-hotel-type accommodation, as we shall see.

UNOCCUPIED BUILDINGS

Occupied/unoccupied dwellings (above), rooms in occupied/unoccupied dwellings (below)

● Occupied[4]
● Unoccupied

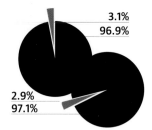

3.1%
96.9%

2.9%
97.1%

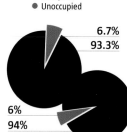

6.7%
93.3%

6%
94%

13.9%
86.1%

12.4%
87.6%

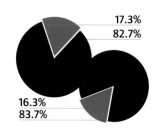

17.3%
82.7%

16.3%
83.7%

The residential building stock used by non-residents

[4] "Unoccupied dwellings" include those used by persons who are domiciled in Venice but not resident.

Only part of the building stock is used for residential purposes and some accommodation is unused either because of its condition or because of the state of the property market.

The only source normally used for measuring the level of use of the housing stock is the population and housing census but this records and provides quantitative information only for buildings used exclusively or predominantly for residential purposes.

From this source, we can nevertheless obtain a general picture of the level of residential use of the building stock.

The census figures show wide variations in the density of residential accommodation in the city in 2001. Santa Croce, Cannaregio and the area between the Rialto Bridge and St Mark's Square had the greatest concentrations of residential accommodation in the city and the highest densities. In the period between the 1971 and 2001 censuses, the total number of dwellings and rooms in the city centre increased slightly, but the proportion occupied by persons resident in the city centre showed a significant decrease. In 1971 officially registered residents occupied 97% of the dwellings and rooms, but this figure fell steadily until, in 2001, residents were occupying only 83% of the dwellings and 84% of the rooms.

People domiciled but not resident; those who live in the historic city for at least part of their time for work, study or pleasure, in fact, use some of the dwellings and rooms shown as "unoccupied". In 2001, this accounted for 874 dwellings, or 2.5% of the total.

For more recent years, we can draw on another source - data from electricity supply contracts.

These figures show that the domiciled, as opposed to resident, proportion of the population has been increasing steadily: from 17% in 1995 to 22% in 2001, reaching 27% in 2007 (see Demography Chapter).

ACTIVE USERS OF ELECTRICITY
By type of contract .

● Resident
● Non-resident

Resident	Non-resident	Year
72.7%	27.3%	2007
74.6%	25.4%	2006
75.4%	24.6%	2005
77.9%	22.1%	2004
76.8%	23.2%	2002
77.6%	22.4%	2001
80.3%	19.7%	1998
79.2%	20.8%	1997
81.2%	18.8%	1996
82.9%	17.1%	1995

ACCOMMODATION IN THE HISTORIC CITY
Left: hotel accommodation; Right: non-hotel accommodation

● Establishments
● Beds
● Rooms

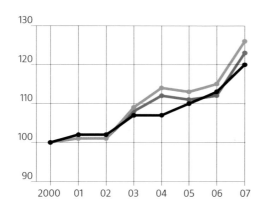
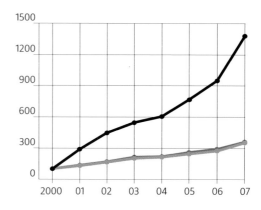

The building stock used by the tourist economy

[5] In Venice the term B&B is usually a euphemism for a dwelling with a small number of rooms to rent and a token breakfast, often delivered by an outside firm. It would be inaccurate to imagine a family catering for a few guests in its domestic setting.

Tourist accommodation in the centre of Venice is plentiful and varied and in recent years both hotel-type and, especially, non-hotel-type facilities have increased. According to the Provincia di Venezia classification, non-hotel-type accommodation comprises rented rooms, holiday houses and apartments, youth hostels, religious institutions offering hospitality, residential study centres, guest rooms for tourists and B&B establishments.

Over the period, the number of establishments grew by 20%, beds by 26% and rooms by 23%. The biggest increases occurred between 2006 and 2007: 6%, 10% and 9% respectively.

Given that it is all but impossible to build on virgin land in Venice, we believe that the increases are the result of permission being granted for hotels to expand into, and convert space in, buildings not previously used as hotels.

The same analysis can be performed for non-hotel accommodation. The figures in the following table show that there has been an explosion of B&Bs[5], rented rooms, hostels and holiday houses in the city.

This has taken place since 1996, when the then municipal Assesesore all'Urbanistica under Mayor Massimo Cacciari, Roberto d'Agostino, lifted the restrictions on the change of use of residential property. There was a time-lag before this became operative, but its effects have been very marked.

One of the most striking statistics is the exceptional jump in just seven years from 142 to 1408 in the number of non-hotel-type establishments, an increase of 1,008 per cent. There were also huge rises in the number of beds (+250 per cent) and rooms (+260 per cent).

[6] The loss may be considerably greater. A survey conducted for the Osservatorio Casa of the Comune di Venezia, Indagine strutture ricettive extralberghiere: Indagine sui siti web (July 2008) showded that there was a 22 per cent discrepancy between the number of rooms to rent and B&BS advertised on the web and the number officially authorized by the Provincia

Annually, this equates to an average rise of 42 per cent in establishments and approximately 20 per cent in the number of beds and rooms.

The large increase in non-hotel accommodation cannot be ascribed exclusively to the opening of new B&B or rooms-to-rent, though they do account for a large proportion.

In July 2008, the Comune of Venice published the findings of a survey (below) in conjunction with Sistema (a research company) of non-hotel-type establishments registered with the Provincial Tourism Office between 2004 and 2008. This showed a virtually constant increase for three types of accommodation – furnished accommodation (average annual increase, 29 per cent), B&Bs (up almost 20 per cent annually) and rooms-to-rent (up almost 5 per cent annually).

The figures are strong ammunition for those worried about the rate of the loss of traditional residential accommodation and its conversion for use by visitors[6]. The Assessorato delle Politiche della Residenza of the Comune says that 44 per cent of the non-hotel accommodation opened in 2001-2007—420 habitations—have been restructured in such a way as to make them unsuitable for domestic living.

NON-HOTEL ACCOMMODATION
In the historic city

● Furnished apartments
● B&Bs
○ Rooms to rent

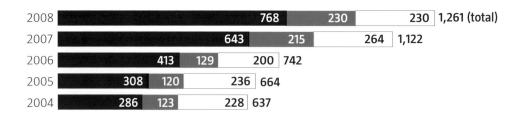

Year	Furnished apartments	B&Bs	Rooms to rent	Total
2008	768	230	230	1,261 (total)
2007	643	215	264	1,122
2006	413	129	200	742
2005	308	120	236	664
2004	286	123	228	637

5
CONCLUSIONS

There has been particularly rapid change in the uses to which buildings in the centre of Venice are put, the inevitable consequence of the growth in tourism and the growth of businesses catering for them.

Public intervention to regulate this situation does not appear to have gone further than declarations of intent. The lack of results is probably the fault of the legislative and regulatory systems, and an absence of incisive measures.

There has been an extraordinary growth of non-hotel accommodation; the least regulated section of the hospitality industry, where barriers to breaking into the market are very low indeed. There is no point in their applying for change of use as the owners do not even need to formally register as running a business. The start-up costs are lower, due partly to the characteristics of the buildings concerned, partly to the fewer rules they need to satisfy. The difference in the prices charged by full-blown hotels and the non-hotel type is much less than the difference between the start-up and management costs of the two types of business. Therefore, what has happened, under the present regulatory conditions, is simply what was bound to happen.

The call for more regulation of new non-hotel accommodation is argued for particularly strongly by the hotel industry, which sees itself as disadvantaged, though for a long time hotels have enjoyed high incomes as a result of restrictions on the development of new rivals in the historic centre.

Another argument debated for years by planners and politicians is whether it would be desirable to create a more normal economic and social mix – more typical of other cities – in Venice, and whether it would be appropriate to prevent changes of use in order to achieve this objective.

In our view, specialisation in cities, or in parts of cities, is a phenomenon common to many other places of importance like Venice. This should not be opposed, even if it were possible. It would

seem more useful to manage the consequences of specialisation and, on these terms, tackle the problem of regulating the use of space and buildings.

Any public policy to regulate the use of buildings must be based on consideration of the economic development of the historic city. This is by definition a difficult task, and particularly difficult to perform with the existing regulations. And it could become even more difficult in the future.

The Veneto Regional Council is currently discussing a new regional law for tourism, that would further reduce the Comune of Venice's room for manoeuvre. The draft legislation reaffirms that the running of family-managed hospitality businesses – B&Bs and rented furnished apartments – does not require a change in the pre-existing residential use of the premises.

It also relaxes certain constraints:
- It allows hotels and those who rent rooms to have annexes located more than 200m from the main building;
- It allows an exemption from the legal requirements governing the minimum height of rooms if the B&B business occupies buildings constructed before 5 July 1975.

Approval of this new regional law governing tourism would please both hotel owners, enabling them to expand their activities without being limited to doing so on the same or adjacent premises, and non-hotel operators, allowing them to convert rooms which, on account of their height, cannot be used as normal living accommodation. This would lift two constraints on the development of accommodation but further tie the hands of public regulators.

Between 2000 and 2007, 41 new hotels opened in Venice.
Since an hotel requires a largish building, and since most of the larger domestic buildings in Venice are patrician buildings, often of great architectural interest and always listed - therefore under the control of the Superintendency for Architecture - their conversion would have been overseen by a superintendent. The Superintendency was, however, unable to give us a list of which palazzi had become hotels, so the architectural historian Leo Schubert compiled an ad hoc list for the Venice Report, which although not complete, shows the nature of the buildings that have undergone a drastic remodelling inside to accommodate bedrooms and bathrooms en suite. This photo essay illustrates some of them, as well as other historic buildings likely to be developed in the future

© Sarah Quill

Palazzo Rava Giustinian
Grand Canal. Was offices of the
ACTV, which runs the vaporetti
Sold by the Comune and has
become an hotel.

© Sarah Quill

Palazzo Soranzo Piovene
Grand Canal. Was office.
Sold by the Comune.
Now an hotel

© Sarah Quill

Palazzo Nani Mocenigo
Rio di Cannaregio, ex offices of
the CNR.
Sold by the Comune. To
become an hotel.

© Sarah Quill

Palazzo Garzoni
Grand Canal. Was Faculty of
Languages of the Università
Ca' Foscari.
Sold by the university. Now
to be an hotel

Palazzo Corner della Regina
Grand Canal. Ex archive of the
Biennale, which has now moved to
Marghera.
Comune wants to sell.
Future use uncertain.

© Sarah Quill

Palazzo Bernardo
Grand Canal. Used to
house Università Ca'Foscari
Archaeology Library.
Sold to a private buyer.

© Sarah Quill

Palazzo Nani Mocenigo
Dorsoduro. Was the Faculty of
Philosophy.
Sold by the university to a
company owned by one of its
own professors.

© Sarah Quill

Cloister of Santo Stefano
Currently still the tax office.
State wants to sell.

© Sarah Quill

Fondaco dei Tedeschi
Rialto. The main post office.
Now to be a Benetton
super store.

© Sarah Quill

Palazzo dei Camerlenghi
Rialto. Was a court house, whose functions have been transferred to Mestre. State wants to sell.

Fabbriche Nuove
Was a court house, whose functions have been transferred to Piazzale Roma.
State wants to sell.

© Sarah Quill

The Ospedale Civile
Future uncertain now that all major investment is going to the new hospital on the mainland.

© Sarah Quill

Mendicanti complex in San Giovanni e Paolo
Was a retirement home. State wants to sell.

© Sarah Quill

Palazzo Sagredo
On the Grand Canal. Was
private housing.
Now an hotel.

© Sarah Quill

Palazzo Ruzzini Priuli
Santa Maria Formosa. Was
private housing.
Now an hotel.

© Sarah Quill

Palazzo Genovese
On the Grand Canal.
To become an hotel.

Chapter 5
Public funding:
Is the future of Venice
sustainable?

Fabrizio Fracchia
Roberta Agnoletto
Francesca Mattassoglio

- The state has allocated large sums, expected to reach €4.271 billion, to build the flood defence system designed to protect Venice and the lagoon

- Funding for Insula, the vital programme to restore the city's canals and embankments, is in decline and the state has cut loans for other works

- Public funding for the city's physical maintenance is erratic and unpredictable, and its accounting systems are so complex as to be untransparent

- There is urgent need for an informed funding policy taking account of the real economy, long-term development prospects and environmental conditions. Without this, none of the fundamental decisions for the safeguarding of the city can be taken

- The new "environment code" potentially provides legal support for those fighting to preserve Venice

1

INTRODUCTION

What public money does Venice receive, how is it channelled to the city, and, most importantly, will these sums be sufficient to ensure that Venice has a viable and sustainable future?

To start with, this public funding needs to be looked at under two headings: the amount Venice receives as an "ordinary" Italian city; and the amount that it is given because of its "special" status and needs, the most obvious being its

We have tried to analyse the interactions between these two sources of funding, focusing on :
- total funding received by the Venice Comune;
- the sums allocated by Special Laws for the

Ministry of Infrastructure and Transport - Venice Water Authority, concessionary Consorzio Venezia Nuova image archive.

Not romantic. High water in December 2008. The tide reached a height of 156 cm above mean water level. This was the fourth highest tide recorded during the last 30 years. When MOSE is finished such scenes will be of the past

unique situation built on, and constantly threatened by, water.

Essentially, the first category of funding is determined by the general legislation applicable to all Italian local government, while the second is governed by laws passed specifically to help Venice.

But analysis is complicated by the fact that the way the city is run is part of a multi-tiered system of government. Some services are run and paid for by the state, others by the region (Veneto), and others by the Venice Comune, (Municipality).

protection of Venice;
- a specific project, Insula, the company established in 1997 and owned by the municipality to repair and carry out maintenance of the city's canals, bridges and foundations.

We also address another important question that is bound up with the multi-layered system of funding. It involves the way funds are used. From a reading of the legislation, it is not immediately clear how sums allocated are actually assigned and spent[1].

[1] All data derives from the official web sites of the authorities concerned and from information provided by Armando Danella, adviser to the Mayor of Venice and the Comune's former Director of Initiatives for the Protection of Venice.

2
THE LEGISLATIVE FRAMEWORK

The goal of protecting and safeguarding Venice is shared by all layers of government: the state, the region and, at municipal level, the Comune of Chioggia as well the Comune of Venice, has a stake in the lagoon.

Venice's unique nature and its national and international importance have prompted the Italian parliament to issue a significant number of special laws over the last three decades to deal with the city's most pressing problems. Of particular note are:

● Law 179/1973 (First Special Law), which declared the protection of Venice and the lagoon as being of paramount national interest;

● Law 798/1984 (Second Special Law), initiating projects to safeguard Venice. This led to the creation of the Consorzio Venezia Nuovo (New Venice Consortium), a public/private sector company to investigate the best way of protecting the city from flooding, eventually leading to the MOSE (Modulo Sperimentale Elettromeccanico) project, the construction of mobile barriers between the islands separating the lagoon from the Adriatic to hold back abnormally high tides;

● Law 139/1992, granting additional powers and funds for the initiatives above.

Parliament has also taken repeated action, often through the annual Finance Law (the Budget), to provide project funding for the city. Notably, the MOSE project was included in the Legge Obiettivo (the "Objective Law" for major national infrastructure projects) in 2002 and the Consorzio Venezia Nuova has continued to receive funding for MOSE from central government.

Additionally, a committee established under Law 798/1984 and chaired by the Prime Minister (known as the Comitatone or "Big Committee") has the task of guiding, co-ordinating and monitoring all initiatives to protect Venice.

On top of these special measures, Venice's routine annual funding stream is largely determined (the term "derived funding" is used) at state and regional level. The city, like all municipal authorities, has only limited autonomy to impose taxes and other levies.

It is worth mentioning that Venice Comune contracts out work to private or part-public, part-private enterprises, such as Insula and ACTV (which is responsible for transport) but the municipality's balance sheet only records any profit or loss that they make.

MOBILE BARRIER SITES
An aerial view of the three inlets from the Adriatic into the lagoon where the mobile barriers are being built, at an estimated cost of €4.271 billion

Venice

Lido lagoon inlet

Malamocco lagoon inlet

Chioggia lagoon inlet

Chioggia

3
FUNDING FLOWS MANAGED BY VENICE

The essential rules of Italy's local finance system are set out in the Constitution. While this establishes that the regions, municipalities, provinces and metropolitan cities shall have "revenue and expenditure" autonomy, it also establishes that they shall "set and levy taxes and collect revenues of their own, in compliance with the Constitution and according to the principles of co-ordination of state finances and the tax system".

- But the public finance principles are established by state laws that limit the scope of regional laws and the freedom with which local authorities can operate.
- Essentially, local finance is based, on the revenue side, on substantial state transfers.

To these are added any income linked to a municipality's – limited – financial autonomy and tax-raising capacity, which must be exercised following principles determined by state laws. Since 1990, a number of changes have been introduced to increase local authorities' financial autonomy but these have not substantively altered the situation.

Beside the annual state transfers (or grant allocations) and a municipality's own income, the state may transfer additional sums for particular projects. A local authority may also take out loans but only for investment expenditure.

A local authority's income can therefore be broken down into five main streams or sources.

- Tax revenues (local taxes, levies, special levies and taxes)
- Revenue and capital transfers from the state or region (including contributions and transfers from the EU, international and other public sector bodies)
- Non-tax revenue (income from public services and assets, interest from loans, net profit from subsidiary or part-owned companies, company dividends and state repayments)
- Revenue from disposals, capital transfers and debt recovery (including capital transfers from the state and region and other public bodies)
- Other sources (cash advances, short-term loans, mortgages, bond issues)

The following table and graph show the main sources of income for the Venice Comune (in euros) each year since 2002.

While it is easy to see the main sources of Venice's income, it is not possible to track the Comune's expenditure with anything like the same precision. Because of time lags and because spending on any budget head can be spread over several years, it would require an extremely complex monitoring procedure to check actual expenditure against allocation of funds.

CHANGES IN INCOME
For the Comune of Venice, 2002 to 2007 (in Euros)

- ● Taxes
- ● Transfers
- ● Non-tax
- ● Capital disposals and transfers
- ● Loans

SOURCES OF INCOME
For the Comune of Venice, 2002 to 2007 (in thousands of Euros)

YEAR	TAXES	TRANSFERS	NON-TAX	CAPITAL DISPOSALS AND TRANSFERS	LOANS
2002	275,639	133,238	52,703	47,845	592,937
2003	303,518	121,191	73,747	156,764	276,182
2004	311,893	119,768	72,977	153,091	168,913
2005	283,747	121,684	72,577	142,077	23,289
2006	308,228	121,742	78,991	141,870	176,155
2007	265,938	157,905	112,565	127,241	133,759

57%

Of Venice's income from taxes - or €164,944,308 - was derived from the municipally owned casino in 2005

relationship between current administrative expenditure (for the routine management of the city) and Venice's "special" needs (ie; spending linked to features and needs unique to Venice).

The Comune's current administrative expenditure is broadly met by its first three revenue sources. Around 45-50% (depending on the year) of this revenue is from local taxation, a further 25-50% comes from transfers (from the state and region), and about 20% is from non-tax revenues.

The income from taxation is heavily dependant on revenue from Venice's municipally owned casino (the city earned a total of €164,944,308, or 57% of all its income from taxes, from gamblers in 2005).

Income from the city's share of ICI (Imposta patrimoniale comunale sugli immobili – local property tax) until abolished this year (an electoral promise by Silvio Berlusconi, now Prime Minister) was also significant, contributing some 11% of the city council's expenditure.

The tax revenues, transfers or allocations from the region and state, and the non-tax revenue not only finance obvious current expenditure (administration costs and the provision of public services etc) but also the services delivered by agencies and companies part-owned by the Venice Comune (for example Vesta, a multi-utility which operates the water and sewage services, and ACTV). The non-tax revenues include profits produced by these companies, although the sums are not particularly significant).

It is the last two sources of Venice's income – the money from loans and from capital disposals and transfers – where the picture is less clear and "overlapping" occurs. Some of this income may be used for Venice's routine needs, some for its requirements as a city of special status.

Equally, money allocated to Venice under one of the Special Laws can appear under the normal revenue budget on the Comune's balance sheets. For example, money, sometimes substantial, allocated by a Special Law for safeguarding Venice may simply be listed under "capital transfers from state to region" (see Funding for special projects with Funding from Special Laws).

To understand the resources reaching Venice as an "ordinary" city, we therefore need to break the sums down (in 2007, for example, funding appearing in the Comune's balance sheet that was directly linked to the Special Laws amounted to €29,508,000).

Is it possible to compare Venice's budget with those of other Italian cities? Only up to a point.

With 270,000 inhabitants on the municipal register (which includes the lagoon islands and a large tract of mainland), Venice's revenue in 2005 amounted to about €738 million and expenditure was €732 million.

Florence, with a similar number of residents, received and spent more than €1.1 billion in 2005, a far larger sum (but did not benefit from any extra payments as did Venice under its Special Laws). It should be said, however, that Venice's revenues have fluctuated over time and its number of residents or inhabitants does not really match its "consumption" which is linked, as far as the historic centre is concerned, primarily to tourism and environmental problems.

As a result, it is very difficult to make comparisons and the only conclusion to draw here is that funding should be uncoupled from any reference to the number of inhabitants and should instead take into account the many other special features of Venice.

4
FUNDING LINKED TO THE SPECIAL LAWS: PROBLEMS IN THE SYSTEM

The following sections will analyse funding for Venice for the protection projects (building the MOSE barriers and the Insula canal improvement, dredging and maintenance scheme) under the Special Laws. First, however, it is useful to clarify funding arrangements for public works not carried out directly by the state.

By making a long-term budgetary commitment, or limiti di impegno, the state meets the payment of the interest and capital on loans taken out from a bank by a public body responsible for carrying out work. Payments are made gradually as the project progresses. Interest subsidies only cover the interest component of mortgages.

These long-term commitments by the state to cover loans have been a constant feature for project funding for Venice. Essentially, the mechanism enables the body responsible for works to obtain a loan or mortgage (subject to approval by the CIPE – the Interministerial Committee for Economic

Planning) in order to have immediate access to funds, while the state only needs to pay off a portion of the total sum each year and "spread" the cost over what can be a very long timescale. A liability limit acts as a "boundary line" limiting the burden on the state. The procedure is subject to a public tender process to select the best bank to provide the funding. In practice, the sum of money available to the public body taking out the loan works out at about nine-tenths of the size of the loan authorised.

These details are essential to gain a clear understanding of the figures set out below.

5

FUNDING FOR PUBLIC WORKS IN VENICE UNDER THE SPECIAL LAWS

The following table sets out the loans made under state guarantee for public works projects under a variety of Special Laws passed since 1984. The sums in the chart are maximum authorised loans ie; each total was not necessarily taken up.

The table, which shows the most significant loans authorised up until 2001, does not include any loans for the construction of the MOSE flood defence barrier system. In January 2008, CIPE estimated that the project's total completion cost will be €4.271 billion. As previously mentioned, loans may be authorised by the Special Laws but

for many reasons they may not be fully taken up.

The following tables (which show actual expenditure by the state, or the Consorzio Venezia Nuova as its agent, by the Veneto region, and by the Venice Comune) show the disparity between the size of guaranteed loans available and the proportion drawn down and spent.

LOANS FOR PUBLIC WORKS IN VENICE
By law number and body authorised to

● State
● Veneto
○ Venice
● Other bodies

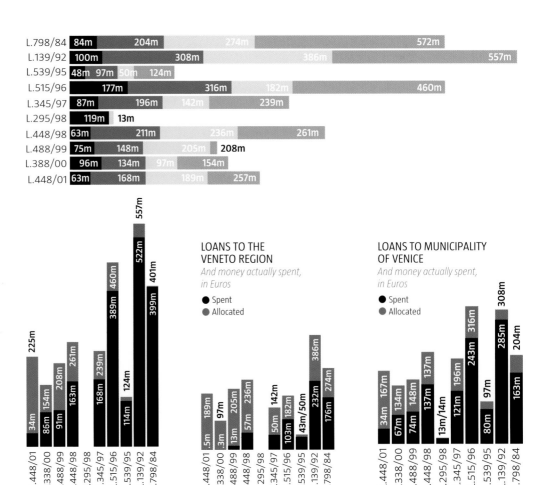

LOANS TO THE STATE/ CONSORZIO VENEZIA NUOVA
And money actually spent, in Euros

● Spent
● Allocated

LOANS TO THE VENETO REGION
And money actually spent, in Euros

● Spent
● Allocated

LOANS TO MUNICIPALITY OF VENICE
And money actually spent, in Euros

● Spent
● Allocated

6

FUNDING FLOWS LINKED TO THE SPECIAL LAWS: INSULA, THE INTEGRATED CANALS PROJECT

Insula is a part-private part-public sector company established in 1997 by the municipality of Venice to take charge of the maintenance, dredging and improvement of the canal system, embankments and bridges, implementing an "integrated canals project" drawn up three years earlier.

By definition, the canal network is essential to Venice and to the sustainability of the activities of the lagoon. Cleaning the canals is also directly linked to the protection of the environment and this integrated approach, managed by a company

December 2008. Special Venetian waders

Ministry of Infrastructure and Transport – Venice Water Authority, concessionary Consorzio Venezia Nuova image archive.

freed from some of the municipal bureaucracy, is scheduled to be in operation for at least 30 years.

Insula benefits from some funding, drawing down loans under the special laws, and successive Finance Laws, as listed below with corresponding sums. More specifically, dredging the canals and maintaining the buildings lining their banks was one of the objectives of Special Law 139/1992, which also proposed grants for private sector bodies. In order to apply this law, a special agreement between state, region and municipality was approved in 1993 to coordinate and integrate resources and initiatives.

Under Special Law 139/1992, 10 per cent of the sums allocated to Veneto Region through the Special Laws must be earmarked for the integrated canals project.

The funding mechanism is similar to the one described earlier. There are limits authorised by law (Laws 139/1992, 515/1996, 448/1998, 388/2000, 448/2001, 296/2006, and 244/2007) under which the municipal authority (or the region) can take out state-guaranteed loans and then allocate this money to the company that will actually be using it.

The funds can be used directly or allocated as grants to private companies carrying out recovery and/or restoration projects as part of the integrated canal strategy.

The sums "committed" and "spent" for this important activity are as follows: at 20/11/2008, €1,724,579,000 had been committed and €1,490,080,000 spent.

It is not possible to identify and analyse all of the countless actions carried out through this project (see following pages on Insula). Suffice to say that the works completed so far have been highly significant, projects such as Insula dei Frari and Insula di Burano and Insula di Santa Maria Formosa.

Venice needs constant, costly maintenance: the vital role of Insula

By Lidia Panzeri

The damage caused by flooding (acqua alta) has an obvious impact on public opinion. A recent case in point was the exceptionally high tide of 1 December 2008 (1.56m above mean water level).

Far less obvious is the long-term threat to Venice: the rising damp that, because of the high degree of salinity, eats into the ancient brick and plasterwork of Venice. And other matters are no less vital to the city's

Water levels are constantly too high in Venice and there is chronic damage to the brickwork and masonry

Katherine Hardy © Venice in Peril

survival and quality of life: maintenance; the dredging and disposal of mud polluted by organic waste (sewage is discharged directly into the canals) and industrial pollutants from nearby Marghera; dealing with subsidence as it affects pavements and foundations, which threatens the stability of buildings; restoring buildings and bridges.

For the most part, this gradual deterioration in the substance of the city cannot be ascribed to the flooding events and therefore does not grab the headlines. It is not registered by public opinion or even the political authorities, but is inherent in the very nature of the city, the alternation of the tides aggravated by the movement of the waves (the increase in the number of powered boats is to blame here), the level of the water in relationship to the buildings, which is chronically too high, due to a combination of subsidence and degradation of the lagoon.

It is perhaps inappropriate to speak of "regular" maintenance, as in Venice any maintenance is exceptional in character. This is the other aspect of what is normally described at safeguarding Venice. The primary aspect, naturally, is defending it against high tides and has led to the MOSE flood defence system, which should be completed in 2014. The two aspects are often seen as mutually exclusive. Some people think, for instance, that it would be sufficient to build up the pavements to 1.20m above mean water level to make the city safe from flooding, while others believe that protecting Venice against extreme high tides will resolve all the city's problems. In reality, the two aspects go hand in hand, and both therefore require special funding.

Regular maintenance, in particular the dredging of canals, should be a never-ending task. This took place in the days of the Venetian Republic, under Austrian domination and after Venice became part of the Italian State. Unfortunately, it was neglected for almost 40 years in the period following the Second World War. One of the reasons for this neglect was the problem of disposing of highly toxic industrial wastes. As a result, some canals became choked up, while buildings and pavements were affected by subsidence.

To deal with these problems, in 1997 the Municipality of Venice created Insula S.p.A. to oversee the necessary maintenance operations. The work itself has been entrusted to specialised firms, most of them locally based.

The various operations proceeded rapidly in the early years, then slowed down when the funds voted under the Special Legislation dried up between 2003 and 2006, being diverted to pay for the mobile barriers. By 2008, the situation was so bad that there were fears the work would be permanently suspended. Fortunately, the government realised that this situation could not continue and has allocated €28 million for further maintenance operations, beginning in 2009.

In the first 10 years of Insula's existence, 338,000 square metres of mud have been dredged, 53 km of canal sides restored, 146,000m^2 of pavement re-laid, and 201 bridges restored. However, 20 km of canals still need to be rehabilitated and 41 km of canal sides, 160 bridges and 340,000m^2 of pavement await restoration.

© Insula Spa

A canal while it is being dredged and its sides repaired by Insula

It is inappropriate to speak of 'regular' maintenance, as in Venice any maintenance is exceptional in character

What do these figures tell us? Where the canal sides are concerned, says Giampaolo Sprocati, chairman of Insula S.p.A, half of the work has now been done, but the whole project will not be completed until 2030.

Two important points: in tandem with the restoration of pavements and bridges, work is being done to renew mains services (water, lighting, gas and fire-prevention networks) and to rebuild the ancient sewage outlets. Another objective is to raise pavements, where possible, so that pedestrians can walk on dry ground even in the case of average-to-high tides (up to 1.20m above mean water level).

These operations involve not only Venice, but also the islands of Murano and Burano, and the Lido. The new operations will be accompanied by a programme of maintenance on the works already done, to avoid having to start again from square one at some time in the future.

Outstanding problems, according to Mr Sprocati, are discontinuity of funding, which makes it impossible to draw up coherent three-year plans, and a lack of coordination between the various agencies (gas and electricity companies), where the mains services are concerned.

One positive development has been Insula's merger, in 2008, with another locally based company, Edilvenezia, which specialises in the restoration of public buildings. This should result in savings of €2 million per annum over the next three years.

7
FUNDING FLOWS FOR MOSE

The construction of the MOSE (Modulo Sperimentale Elettromeccanico) flood defence barriers to protect the lagoon from exceptionally high tides in the Adriatic is by far and away the biggest public works project the city has seen for decades. It makes an enormous call on public money, thereby raising serious questions as to whether other projects and even the routine management of Venice are suffering financially in order that MOSE, a national flagship project, can be completed.

Construction of the barriers and associated works were started by the Consorzio Venezia Nuova (CVN) in 2003 and are currently due for completion between 2012 and 2014.

The estimated final completion cost is €4.271 billion and a resolution of CIPE (the Interministerial Committee for Economic Planning) disclosed that by December 2007 a total of €2.043 billion had been allocated to the project.

That sum, advanced to CVN in tranches since 1984, is broken down in the table below.

The CIPE resolution of January 2008 added that, by December 2007, €1,662,390,000 (some 39% of the total cost of the project) was committed in the form of works completed, in progress or about to start. Completed expenditure amounted to €1,510,180, 000. According to the resolution, the amount remaining to be financed was €2,228,630, 000.

MOSE FUNDING
Breaking down the €2.043bn allocated by Dec. 2007

MEASURE	FUNDING (€m)
Funding under Law 798/1984	111.73
Objective Law and CIPE Res. 2002/2003	50
Objective Law and CIPE Res. 2004	638.1
Objective Law and CIPE Res. 2006	380
Objective Law and CIPE Res. 2007	243.17
Increase in borrowed capital, CIPE Res. 2007	50
Decree Law 2007	170
Finance Law 2007 and CIPE Resolution 2008	400

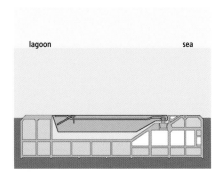

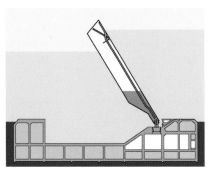

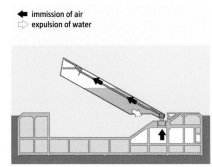

immission of air
expulsion of water

Katherine Hardy © Venice in Peril

Advertising in public spaces

Renata Codello, superintendent for architecture in Venice, says, "I have no choice: in 2007 some of the marble facing of the Doge's Palace fell down; in 2008 it was a bit of the cornice of the Correr. Under law I am personally responsible if a tourist gets hurt. With the cuts to our funding [25.8% in 2009] I can expect no help from government."

Until recently, one of the many extraordinary aspects of Venice was that it was a city with almost no advertising. Now, however, the agencies dealing in mega-advertising locations have realised they can exploit a recent change in the law to sell space there and make a large profit, yet they still get called sponsors by the authorities. The law allows the scaffolding on public buildings (which includes all churches as these are maintained by the state) under restoration to carry advertising so long as the superintendent considers that it does not "detract from the appearance, decorum or public enjoyment of the building".

While the existing ads in Venice have aroused local and international protest, Dr Codello insists that she has been very discriminating: "I have turned down masses of proposals, including one with the entire Italian football team dressed only in their shorts", she told the Association of Private Committees for Venice in October 2008. Despite the downturn in the economy, the number of ads keeps growing as international agencies such as Plakativ Media realise that Venice is a rich market in which to promote products.

8
CONCLUSIONS

Because the financial governance of Venice is based on a multi-annual funding mechanism, it is not easy to see or understand the costs incurred in running the city.

Public authorities should be encouraged to disseminate improved and more digestible data in order for there to be better debate about financial priorities and the problems facing Venice.

The state and its concessionary company, the Consorzio Venezia Nuova, play a decisive role in the financial condition of the city. This is recognition that the Republic as a whole must take responsibility for this unique conurbation and is in keeping with the "upward subsidiarity" approach that requires support from the higher levels of government when the lower ones cannot take care of local interests.

Though it is hard to foresee the protection of Venice being entrusted to some abstract global authority, we can see a financial role for the EU, whether directly or through the European Investment Bank.

One of the big questions facing the city is whether the huge cost – currently projected to be a total of €4.271 billion — of MOSE, the flood defence system, is being met by diverting funds from elsewhere, from other projects in Venice or from routine services.

The evidence that this is so is unclear. In recent years, the Venice Comune's revenue and expenditure has remained roughly stable, at around €750 million per annum, though it has increased (sometimes considerably) in certain years.

But it is evident that there has been a decline in the loans made available to the city under the Special Laws since funding for MOSE began. In 2002, Venice drew down €592 million under this arrangement. In 2005, the figure dropped to just €23 million although it had picked up to €133 million in 2007.

Since 1984, a total of around €7.55 billion has been allocated to Venice under Special Laws and successive Finance Laws.

Looking to the future, the abolition of the local property tax, ICI, will lead to a reduction in municipal revenues (in 2007, for example, ICI brought in €64 million), though this may be offset by an increase in the annual state transfers. In reality, the ICI rate in Venice has traditionally been low and income from it has been supplemented by revenues from the Casino. However, the Casino is currently proving less profitable than in the past.

State transfers have also been influenced recently by Italy's compliance, as an EU member country, with the Stability Pact, which requires improvements in member states' budgetary positions. These restrictions will continue into the future. As to Insula, the integrated canals maintenance project, it is clear that funding needs to be long term. It is scheduled to run for 30 years at an estimated cost of €1.2 billion. But funding allocations have decreased in recent years, a trend that entails inevitable problems and it is apparent that the public authorities will need to continue to take responsibility for the problem beyond the first 30-year period.

It is beyond argument that funding Venice must give due consideration to our duty to future generations. It is only through sustainable development that these generations can be assured of an opportunity to benefit from the cultural, environmental and historic heritage of the city.

It is by no means easy to translate this need into concrete reality. Today, however, a legal instrument does exist. Article.3 of Legislative Decree 152/2006 (as amended by Legislative Decree 4/2008), known as the "environment code", envisages that "every human activity legally relevant under the present code must conform to the principle of sustainable development in order to ensure that satisfying the needs of the present generation does not compromise the quality of life and opportunities of future generations".

The decree goes on to say that "the activity of the public administration must also be conducted in such a way that the principle of sustainable development can be implemented in the best possible manner. For this reason, in comparative choices involving public and private interests over which there is a degree of discretion, priority must be given to the interests of protecting the

Though it is hard to foresee the **protection of Venice** being entrusted to some **abstract global authority**, we can see a financial role for the **EU**, directly or through the **European Investment Bank**

Ministry of Infrastructure and Transport - Venice Water Authority, concessionary Consorzio Venezia Nuova image archive.

Under the porticoes of St Mark's Square on 1st December 2008. The square is the lowest lying part of the city, only 80cm above mean water level.

environment and the cultural heritage".

The importance of sustainable development seems to have crossed a legal boundary. Citizens may call for this principle to be applied, including before the courts, and if it is given its due weight it could provide new impetus for the protection of Venice.

Once the stock of resources that we are duty-bound to preserve for future generations has been

accurately identified, it should be relatively simple to draw up a catalogue of priorities and to assess the role to be played by public funding.

For this to happen, though, we need to apply skilled manpower to conducting research into the role of funding policy: without a proper awareness of the real economy, long-term development prospects and environmental conditions, we cannot take the fundamental decisions.

How the Dutch manage and finance their flood protection

By Francesca Mattasoglio

Water management is an absolute priority for the Dutch since more than half (55 per cent) of their territory is below sea-level. Over 60 per cent of the population, who produce over 65 per cent of GDP, live on this land. Moreover, Holland needs to defend itself not just from flooding from the North Sea and Waddenzee, but also from the dangers posed by the numerous rivers flowing through the country: notably the Rhine, Maas (Meuse), Scheldt and Ems.

All the Dutch are aware that the perfect working of the country's dykes, dams and water defence systems is a question of life and death, especially now that climate change is increasing the pace at which water levels are rising. For this reason, there is wide public awareness of the vital need for research to find the best possible solution to address new needs while balancing the various interests at stake. The water protection policy described here was introduced after the disastrous flood of 1953, which affected most of the provinces of Zeeland and South Holland, causing serious damage to property and leaving more than 1,800 people dead. Since then, a new protection policy has been followed, based on stepping up the

> **Unlike in Italy, there is consistent investment in research, based on five-year planning and funding systems**

construction of dykes and dams in the affected areas to hold back the North Sea, and on implementing defences along the Western Scheldt and in the Rotterdam area. The Minister of Transport, Public Works and Water Management established a Delta Committee, which draw up a series of measures known as the Delta Plan. These were transposed to the Delta Act of 1958.

The current water management policy is based on three pillars:
- Legislation
- Institutional and financial organisation
- Science and technology

How the authorities divide up their responsibilities
- State
- Directorate General Water Affairs: deals with policing and budget
- Directorate General Public Works and Water Management: deals with planning, construction and maintenance of primary defences and closed barriers.

- Provinces: Water issues and special planning
- Water boards: Maintenance of secondary defences; safety assessments; planning and construction of secondary defences.

Holland has two types of water defence projects:
- Primary works
- Secondary works

Primary works are the most important initiatives defending the country from the North Sea. Given the vast areas concerned, their cost and the considerable technical expertise required to design and construct them, these works are the responsibility of the state since they are deemed to be of national importance. Primary works are financed from national funds, albeit in competition with any other national priorities.

Secondary works are the sole responsibility of the Water Boards.

The Water Boards

The Water Boards are local public bodies (at present numbering 37) established specifically for water management. Their members are elected democratically.

Their tasks include:
- Water protection: infrastructure maintenance (dykes, dams and dunes)
- Water management: both quantitative (drainage, irrigation, monitoring and maintaining appropriate water levels); and qualitative (combating water pollution and implementing surface-water quality measures)
- Urban wastewater treatment
- Maintenance, on occasion, of inland pipelines and rural roads.

To carry out their tasks, the Dutch Water Boards have a self-financing system based on their own tax-raising powers. These encompass:
- Water system tax (for flood protection)
- Water pollution levy (for wastewater treatment and water quality management).

These taxes enable the costs borne by the Water Boards to be covered more or less in full.

Whenever external funding is needed, the Boards can apply to the Nederlandse Waterschapsbank N.V., a bank set up specifically for this purpose at a time when they were not allowed to apply to private banks for loans.

Financing

At the national level, the annual budget amounts to €500 million. Studies suggest that by the end of 2020 a further €5-6 billion will be necessary.
- €806 million for flood protection measures as